UNTYING THE KNOTS BEFORE TYING THE KNOT:
Things To Reflect On Before You Take the Vow

ROSE ENYIOMA

Copyright © 2016 Rose Enyioma

All rights reserved.

ISBN: 0-9896377-5-1
ISBN-13: 978-0-9896377-5-6

DEDICATION

This book is dedicated to my eldest sister, Dr. (Mrs.) Doris, Inko-Tariah who taught me how to read and encouraged me to become an avid reader and a writer.

CONTENTS

ACKNOWLEDGMENTS i

Chapter 1: Unlocking the Past 1

Chapter 2: Marriage License Requirements… or Not! 7

Chapter 3: The Origin of Marriage 15

Chapter 4: Perception of Marriage 23

Chapter 5: Who we are 29

Chapter 6: Know Yourself 33

Chapter 7: What the Bible Says You Are 39

Chapter 8: New in Christ 47

Chapter 9: Changing Paradigms 53

Chapter 10: Putting Your Life on Hold 61

Chapter 11: Power of Little Things 67

Chapter 12: Expectations 73

Chapter 13: Prejudices 83

Chapter 14: "Shopping" and "Choosing" 89

Chapter 15: Philosophy of Life 99

Chapter 16: Definition of a Successful Marriage 103

Chapter 17: The Last Chapter 107

Chapter 18: Oh! Just One More Thing 111

ABOUT THE AUTHOR 117

ACKNOWLEDGMENTS

To my husband, Ike, and my children, Michael, Hannah, who typed the script, and Jesse, who encouraged me to finish.

To my late parents, Nze Michael and Mrs. Christiana Obute, who made me understand that hard work and persistence are the ways to achieve goals.

To my other siblings, Pastor (Mrs.)Theo Anyawnu, Mrs. Terry Nwokoroku, Prof Gordian Obute, and the late Mrs. Augusti Onyekonwu, if I had to choose my siblings again, I will always choose you all.

My special thanks go to my brothers-in-law, Prof. Mike Onyekonwu and Pastor Festus Anyawnu, for being there. To my sisters-in-law, Aunty Helen, late Aunty Jane, Ariochi, Ruth, and all of Jonathan Enyioma's family, I thank you for receiving me with open hands.

To the Onyenezis, I say thanks for opening your home to me when you didn't have to. Pastor and Mrs. Nwuba saw something in me when I did not know it existed. Mrs. Nwuba saw and encouraged the gift of God in me and has been my cheerleader. She listened to my ideas when they did not make sense to others. To the spiritual mothers and sisters, Pastors Vero Ebie and Victoria Emmanuel, thanks for your motherly counsel. To Augusta Oparaku, Pastor Jane Afiesimama, and Brother Jonathan Ebiziem, thanks for encouraging me to stay with it and not totally give up.

I also thank my editor, Melanie Saxton, for her encouragement, advice and keen eye. She said, "This is what the world is missing — a formula for "old-fashioned" love." I hope my readers feel the same.

Chapter 1:
Unlocking the Past

Whether your great-grandparents came from Europe, Africa, Asia or the Andes, I can almost guarantee that most of them faced the harshest obstacles. They overcame war, poverty, disease, lack of technology and education, and a host of other challenges. Some lived in third world conditions, yet through it all, they stayed married and raised families. It's as though those terrible conditions brought them closer... like a team pulling on the same rope to win (or in this case, survive).

"First World" Problems

Ironically, today we face "first world" problems, which seem to be harder on marriages than the third world stresses! So why, exactly, do our "first world" problems pull modern couples apart? Perhaps it's because people are operating blindly without an "instruction manual." Our ancestors read the manual, but couples today have misplaced it. Or they ignore it. As old fashioned as it sounds, the Bible is an excellent instruction manual for marriages. It lights the path and points the way, so it's no surprise older generations leaned on their faith. They believed in a higher power and prayed their way through. And they stayed married. And so can today's couples. As you are getting ready to walk the aisle, it is good to decide where you will base your union.

What's Old is New Again

Does this mean we have to live as antiquated relics of a bygone era? No, not at all. No one is saying you should wear a bonnet or drive a horse and buggy. You don't need a chaperone to go on a date. It's the ethics we should mirror. It's the internal (and eternal) sense of right, wrong, balance and imbalance. Our grandparents and great grandparents had fine-tuned moral compasses. We should pay attention to that!

Personally, I wanted what they had — stability, trustworthiness, courage, decency, honor and a huge focus on the family. I am one of the fortunate people who is trying to intertwine yesterday's wisdom with today's modern, fast-paced life. It's all in the recipe. My marriage is "cooked" in butter, rather than non-stick spray. There are many just like me who are trying to enjoy married life and sustain it through a lot of hard work, mutual respect, irreplaceable roles, and shared values — lifelong ingredients that feed a marriage.

Not that we don't occasionally burn a pork chop... but we keep a little extra arsenal in our back pocket that allows us to savor it, regardless. This arsenal includes a belief system that is as timeless today as it was then.

Listen To Your Great-Grandmother… Not MSNBC

We live in a time when almost everything is relative. Our culture is soaked in moral relativism, and what used to shock us to the core has become an everyday occurrence and part of normal conversation! Let's face it. Every facet of our lives is controlled by the liberal media. Unfortunately, we are bombarded with news from around the world that attempts to reshape our world-view.

That's a problem our ancestors didn't have… and their successful marriages prove it. Remember, their marriages were founded on a conventional world-view. They didn't have media bias diluting the gravity of some of our most important issues. They didn't live through the redefinition of families, couples and marriage.

Most of us just shrug off current events, believing they don't affect us. But they do. This constant march toward an "altered reality" undercuts the importance our ancestors placed on traditional relationships.

Absolutes... Absolutely!

Many successfully married soul-mates share a Christian belief system and look to the Bible as their guide. No matter the backlash against traditional values, the fact remains that God's word binds and blesses couples. Liberals may accuse Christians of being knuckle-dragging, stone-aged, myth-believing Neanderthals, but that doesn't erase historic truths. The Left may mock the sanctity of traditional marriage... but that doesn't make it less sacred or less successful. It's time for we Christians to hold our heads high and proclaim, "Our beliefs work miracles in marriages!" Can non-believers say that about their belief system? Hmmm?

I sometimes wonder about what people two generations hereafter will be like. To save them, we have to go back and reacquaint ourselves with "absolutes." I have found that the value systems of older married couples stem from absolutes, which, most times, are diametrically opposed to the age of relativism we live in. The results of our relativistic thinking has dealt the marriage institution a crushing blow.

For instance, the eternal word of God is absolute. But the younger generations tend to think that whatever feels valid to us is our reality. If it feels pleasant, it is okay to do it. Really? The consequences of some of the things that "feel good" could be very devastating a few short years later and possibly irreversible. Then we begin to think about what could have been, and we decide to blame everyone except ourselves. Sound familiar?

Good is Always the Enemy of Best

An acquaintance of mine has a brilliant son who was enrolled in a magnet school. He received a full-ride scholarship to Yale University and many other colleges others are yearning to attend. At the age of eighteen, he refused the scholarships and instead found a job in a shop, where he earned just above minimum wage. He acquired an apartment, a beat-up car, and a child along the way. When he was in his mid-twenties, he saw all the former classmates he used to help beginning to graduate and making double and triple what he was being paid. It was then that he realized his grave mistake and enrolled in a community college.

What if he had accepted the scholarship to Yale and didn't have to pay for college? What if he had graduated from college within four to five years and started a high-paying career in his mid-twenties? Think about it. This story ended well because this gentleman came to his senses. He could ultimately re-write his destiny and redeem the time he lost. He changed his trajectory. He finally accepted an absolute: education matters. This is a happy ending because he was smart enough to accept his mistake and had the gumption to change his life.

How does the young man's story resonate in a Christian marriage setting? Well, this man would have, perhaps, made a different decision if anyone in his family had been to college. But his family focused on work rather than higher education. His grandfather, a very hardworking man, labored in a manufacturing plant for over forty years. He had a home and a respectable level of income compared to his peers. His grandmother also worked with a high school diploma for years. His mother, aunts, and uncles were all high school graduates. He was going to be the first in the family to go to college.

We can safely say that if this young man had a very strong college role model, he would have chosen differently. But he grew up in a family where hard work was emphasized, and he followed the same pattern. On the surface this is good, but good is always the enemy of best.

Having strong role models in the area of marriage helps us to think and pattern our lives. In the age of relativism, marriage is no longer the mainstream option. There are now alternatives to marriage with detrimental consequences. Unfortunately, millions are experimenting with "formulas" that are untested. They should be applying what is verified and true, don't you think so?

Rejecting the Social Experiments

Notice how young people are being conditioned to clamor for wealth, fame, and fortune above character and integrity. Our heroes are larger than life, and fans copy their every move. We tend to follow celebrity-opinions on issues—even on the issues they are grossly ignorant about. This has significantly affected the marriage institution.

This book examines the factors prior to marriage that can make or break a union. It brings to light issues that can be addressed upfront and positively impact the marriage relationship. These issues are "knots," and the goal is to "untie" them before couples walk down the aisle. Then they can start their marriages on solid foundations.

So sit back as we detangle the knots with some profound and timeless truths. The goal is to find a much more realistic and balanced approach to marriages… that last.

Think about it.

Older marriages lasted because they valued old fashioned biblical principles, rooted in the fear of God; and were not affected by the distractions of today.

In our age of relativism, anything that makes us feel good becomes our reality. Sometimes this leads us to self-destruction.

Chapter 2:
Marriage License Requirements... Or Not!

Marriage is the oldest institution in the history of mankind, yet it is the only one that does not require a stringent minimum standard. You must have a license to drive a car, motorcycle, boat or 18-wheeler. Likewise, every trade or profession has a required minimum standard that must be achieved prior to practicing it.

For instance, if you want to be a nurse, you have to decide what level you want to attain. There are licensed vocational nurses (LVNs), registered nurses (RNs), and baccalaureate nurses; from there you can advance to PhD level. Some start by being certified nurse assistants.

Whatever level you choose, there are conditions and requirements you must meet before you are issued a license by the Board of Nursing in your state. In my state of Texas, you are also required to maintain that license by getting at least twenty continuing education credit units (CEUs) before you can renew your license every two years. This helps refresh your knowledge and keeps you informed of relevant advancements in nursing. It also keeps the public safe, since only those who maintain their licenses will keep practicing. If you do not keep up with your education, you lose your license.

Unprepared and Rudderless

Unfortunately, marriage is the sole institution where the minimum requirement is eighteen years of age, or lower if you are an emancipated youth or live in a state with a reduced age of consent. This results in two people joining their lives and futures without an idea of how to "set sail," let alone navigate the highs and lows of marriage. They find themselves rudderless in life's storms. Put another way, their lack of preparation is a recipe for failure, because they do not know how to "nourish" their marriage with the necessary ingredients.

The story is further complicated when these unprepared husbands and wives have children. Children deserve to be raised by adults, but are being raised by clueless parents who are more or less children themselves. Chronological age may not be a factor for maturity because there are some properly rounded twenty-one year-old adults… and adolescent forty-year-old "kids." Sadly, it's a game of chance for their offspring, who may or may not have parents who are worthy to be emulated.

Confusion and Complications

With the recent legalization of same sex-marriage, it is now "okay" for anyone to marry anyone. I realize there are other forms of the union in our relative world, but this book is geared toward Biblical marriage. This is an absolute concept where one man marries one woman at a time. Period.

Unfortunately, there is no education or standard preparation for marriage, unless a couple seeks counseling, takes a class, or talks to their pastor or priest. Some churches have mandatory premarital counseling classes before a wedding is conducted. But do all churches do that? No. And some only touch the tip of the iceberg, without really excavating the ice. Lack of preparation can turn a marriage into a disaster of "Titanic" proportions.

In reality, how many independent young people still go to church in the first place, and what is the percentage when compared to the larger population? More often than not, young couples mimic what they have learned from the adults in their lives: grandparents, parents, pastors, church members, neighbors, or parents of their friends. Some get their marriage licenses from the justice of the peace. Some elope to Las Vegas. Others live in a "common law" state of marriage with no license or ceremony at all. It's like the United States has become a laboratory of marriage experimentation, with society shunning the "old fashioned" virtues upon which the nation was built. Again, we have a lost and rudderless collection of marriage failures.

Couples who base their marriage on what they have learned from their role models are at the mercy of that example. The danger is that couples simply have not been exposed to the right perspective or biblical view of marriage. If young men and women have been indoctrinated with erroneous facts up-front, how can they possibly realize what is inaccurate?

Marriage is NOT a Way Out

The marriage institution is the bedrock of society. The condition of the marriage institution reflects the larger community. People should have a certain level of confidence when they walk down the aisle. They deserve to know what does and doesn't work, and what to expect up-front. Ideally, they should marry for the right reasons: love, shared interests, and above all a Christ-centered focus on the future.

But with the divorce rate out of control, this obviously is not the case. Several myths and falsehoods abound about the institution, and people who believe these myths go into marriage with serious knowledge-handicaps. For instance, there may be peer pressure. When a young man or woman see their friends tie the knot, the temptation is to join the crowd. Or sons and daughters may experience intense pressure from their parents to get married, especially in traditional societies. They may get an ear-full about who has just gotten married and be coerced with loaded questions, such as: "When are you going to give me grandchildren?"

Others marry without being ready simply to escape problems at home. This happens more often in blended families and when there are addictions or abuse in the home, where little children forfeit their childhood because the adults have problems. So many wounded young people believe marriage is a "way out" of the turmoil, not realizing that they have just leapt from the frying pan into the fire. They find themselves married without the tools to break the cycles of chaos and are doomed to repeat them.

Some marry because they are lonely. This is the wrong mindset, because some of the loneliest people are married people, and they have become caught in a trap. It is rather better that lonely persons to first find their place in the world, their place in a church home, and a place where they can volunteer and give back. How much better that they trust God to place a soul mate in their path… even when the wait is long. Easier said than done? Absolutely. But some of the most vibrant marriages are long awaited — and highly successful — because two mature and stable people waited patiently before being joined together by the master match maker.

Others retreat to marriage because of pregnancy. They try to do the right thing. Some are forced into this due to their parents' pledge or societal obligations. A "shotgun wedding" comes to mind, and is often followed by divorce — a sad ending to a desperate and guilt-riddled situation.

It doesn't have to be this way. None of the scenarios above is a cause to enter into marriage… unless the groundwork has been properly laid. Men and women both need "marriage education" to survive — and thrive — as couples.

From Bad to Worse

I happened to watch an episode of Divorce Court where a woman was seeking monetary compensation from a younger man from whom she had separated. When they discussed the issues, the lady stated that the main reason she married him was because he fulfilled her sexually. She already had two children by another man and had one child with this man. She was also frustrated that he was not measuring up financially, so much that she had an intimate relationship with her ex, who gave her money to buy gas on her wedding day to this man she was currently separated from. The judge was appalled by the woman's admission and stated: "Who does that? Who marries one man and sleeps with another man on her wedding day?"

If you are considering marriage simply because of sexual chemistry, please stop. Marriage is much more complex than sex. This is not to diminish the role of sex in a marriage relationship.

However, if that is the only reason you are heading down the aisle, you are on a slippery slope. Sex, alone, is an erroneous premise that will trip you up.

We are not animals. We are human beings comprised of Spirit, soul body and spirit. Truly, we are "spiritual beings on a human journey" rather than "human beings on a spiritual journey." There is much more to us than just the physical. Our intellectual and soulful components are as important — if not more important — than our physical bodies. Marriage is meant to minister to the whole person. And when the Lord heads the union, it is possible to overcome any obstacle that threatens to tear couples apart. Remember this as you contemplate your future spouse. Is this the man or woman God wants for you? Or is the man or woman "you" want, regardless of God's divine plan?

Have patience. Have virtue. Your mate awaits.

Knowledge is Power

Some marriages do not always lead to "happily ever". We know this, but how easy it is to see our significant other through rose-colored glasses. When caught up in a whirlwind romance, it is easy to forget that people have suffered an untimely death at the hands of a spouse. Some live in a "dysfunction junction" without ever knowing what a Christ-centered marriage is like. These are the unfortunate realities.

Yes, knowledge is power. Know yourself. Know Jesus. Welcome the Father's guidance. Reject feelings of loneliness and desperation, and believe that you will be joined with your soulmate in God's good timing. And while you are at it, learn as much as you can about "old-fashioned" love (this book is a good start)! Study successful marriages. Study the values of your elders. Study the long-term unions that thrived in various cultures. Let your marriage be built on genuine love and nothing else. This is the only way you and your spouse will weather the storms of life… successfully.

Think about It.

Marriages last when we marry for the right reasons. A marriage where the two partners are mature and prepared has a better chance of lasting for life.

The marriage institution is the bedrock of society. The condition of the marriage institution reflects the larger community.

ROSE ENYIOMA

Chapter 3:
The Origin of Marriage

What Is Marriage?

Marriage has been defined by different entities, including Webster's Dictionary:

A. the state of being married

B. the mutual relationship between husband and wife

C. The institution whereby a man and a woman are joined in a special kind of collective and legitimate dependence for founding and maintaining a family.[1]

Of course, there's more to marriage than a "definition" out of a secular dictionary. Christians have the benefit of a Biblical definition : a spiritual union based on love, respect, devotion and mutual beliefs.

Right is Wrong and Wrong is Right?

As mentioned in the previous chapter, just recently the Supreme Court of the United State redefined marriage to include same-sex unions, leaving most of the Christian population in shock. The law of the land no longer reflects the Biblical and timeless institution of man-woman, husband-wife. This "politically correct" and tragic attempt to deconstruct the family flies in the face of time- honored Christian ethics. It certainly does not mirror the wisdom of our ancestors who populated planet-Earth with

---

[1] http://www.merriam-webster.com/dictionary/marriage.

God-ordained male-female marriages.

A tiny percentage of Americans benefit from same-sex unions. But their relentless lobby against Christian values has been extremely vocal… and quite successful. They have managed to topple the cornerstone of family infrastructure dating back to Genesis, all the while "shaming" others who do not agree with their social experimentation. They throw verbal bombs at their critics, calling us "homophobic" or "unenlightened" when we grieve the loss of Christian traditions. So what are we to do about it?

God's View on the Matter

Always remember, we did not make the rules. God made the rules, and blessings flow to those who respect and cherish his holy word… and the holy state of traditional matrimony. Stand firm on timeless principles.

For this discussion, we will define marriage as a covenant between God, man, and woman performed by the church, state, or individuals recognized by the state. It is primarily a union between God and two individuals who have spiritual, cultural, and lawful rights. It is a contract and bond between a man and a woman with God's direct involvement — an arrangement that allows two incomplete persons to complete each other as one entity. As a divine plan, it achieves the following:

- ❖ Procreation and formation of a family unit
- ❖ Security and enhancement of economic status
- ❖ Enhancement of social standing in the community
- ❖ Legal decision- making
- ❖ Public declaration of love and the right and enticement to sexual partnership
- ❖ Fulfillment of family or religious obligations or to gain citizenship of another nation

In the Beginning

For Christians, marriage started back in Genesis, or the book of the beginning. The biblical account states that God made light on the first day, evening and morning on the second day, vegetation and fruits on the third day, the sun and moon on the fourth day, and great creatures and living things on the fifth day. On the sixth day, the following happened:

God said, "Let us make man in our own image, after our own likeness, and let them rule over the fish of the sea and the birds of the air, over the livestock, over all the earth, and over all the creatures that move along the ground." So God created man in his own image, in the image of God, he created him; male and female he created. (Genesis 1:26–27 NIV)

The Lord God said, "It is not good for man to be alone. I will make him a helper suitable for him. …" But for Adam, no suitable helper was found. So the Lord God caused the man to fall into a deep sleep; and while he was sleeping, he took one of the man's ribs and closed up the place with flesh. The Lord God made a woman from the rib he had taken out of the man, and he brought her to the man. The man said, "This is now bone of my bone and flesh of my flesh; she shall be called 'woman' for she was taken out of man. For this reason, a man will leave his mother and father and be united to his wife, and they will become one flesh." (Genesis 2:18, 20–25)

Why did God Ordain the Institution of Marriage?

God, who is the author and creator of life, has purposely created us with a void in our lives… a void for him. He is the only one who can fill this deep spiritual need. If we are going into a marriage union thinking it will fill that void, we are mistaken. If anything, marriage makes us realize how much more we need God to fill that void before we can complete and complement our spouses.

Everything that God created is perfect in itself, including marriage. Look at the Book of Malachi 2:15(amp version):

"And did not God make [you and your wife] one [flesh]? Did not one make you and preserve your spirit alive? And why [did God make you two] one? Because He sought a godly offspring [from your union]. Therefore, take heed to yourselves, and let no one deal treacherously and be faithless to the wife of his youth" It is clearly showing here that God wants Godly offspring from marriage union.

There are added benefits. We also see in Ecclesiastes 4:9-12 King James Version (KJV):

"Two are better than one; because they have a good reward for their labor. For if they fall, the one will lift up his fellow: but woe to him that is alone when he falleth; for he hath not another to help him up. Again, if two lie together, then they have heat: but how can one be warm alone? And if one prevails against him, two shall withstand him; and a threefold cord is not quickly broken."

Please, read the article written by Waite - 2003, titled "The Benefits from Marriage and Religion in the United States" at www.ncbi.nlm.nih.gov/pmc/articles/PMC2614329/. Surprisingly, this government link shares compelling evidence that marriage and religion benefit Americans.

The Perfect Marriage?

What does a flawless marriage look like? Hmmm...the husband would be a clone of Absalom, with the added Wisdom of Solomon, the strength of Sampson, the meekness of Moses, the dedication and integrity of Daniel, the patience of Job, and the forgiving heart of Joseph. The wife would have the beauty of Sarah, the wisdom of the women of the town of Abel, and the humanity and gentleness of Mother Theresa. She would cook better than your grandmother and be trained to please a man like a Geisha. When all these components come together, she would be the picture of a Proverbs 31 woman.

There would be no arguments and no misunderstandings in this marriage. Their lives would be perfect. Their children would be perfect. And you probably already realize that there can never be a couple with all of these qualities. There is no perfect human being on earth. Only God is flawless. And because we are all imperfect, there is no such thing as a faultless union. When we understand this, it will help us relate better with other people. Rather than looking for a perfect union, we should accept each other and expect to be loved just the way we are.

Double Standards

Problems develop when we expect our spouses to understand and overlook our weaknesses, while we hold them accountable for their weaknesses. Perhaps we have overinflated expectations. Instead of harping on each other's not-so-good habits, we should focus on what attracted him or her to us in the first place. This makes for a very meaningful relationship — a relationship that doesn't need "fixing." With mutual love and "give and take," the rough spots will be polished as a couple learns to live together.

It is also safe to say that we all put our best foot forward while we are just getting to know our beloved. This paints a less than accurate picture of who we really are, doesn't it? It's no wonder that when the honeymoon ends and the real person emerges, we suddenly face the "knots" that should have been untangled during the courtship!

Be honest. Be transparent. Be yourself. And encourage these concepts as you court a prospective spouse. Assure your significant other that you want to know him or her, warts and all. Only then can couples truly assess their compatibility and prepare for marriage — a special and unique marriage shaped by them and founded on the Lord.

Words to Count On

To have a very meaningful, fulfilling union, we should know the following things:

- ❖ As long as two imperfect people join together, there will be no perfect marriage union.
- ❖ Your marriage will be a result of what you and your spouse decide to make of it. It takes both partners to make that

decision.

- There is a lot of sacrifice of personal perspective for the good of the union.
- Your preparation and perception prior to marriage will heavily affect the success or the lack of it in the union… unless both are flexible and willing to relearn when there is a need to.
- Life is unpredictable; however, if both of you predetermine that this union is for life, you will make it. Emphasis is on both, not one, partner.
- Establishing your definition of marriage will go a long way for you to evaluate your union periodically as you compare it to that definition.
- Most importantly, the one who authored marriage has left a manual on how to make marriage work. If you read and follow the instructions, you will not go wrong.
- Have attainable goals that will help you achieve your working definition of a successful marriage.
- Help other people along the way.
- Be accountable to God individually and corporately for your actions.

Think about it.

Marriage is a God- ordained institution between a man and a woman for life.

Two are better than one; because they have a good reward for their labor. For if they fall, the one will lift up his fellow: but woe to him that is alone when he falleth; for he hath not another to help him up. – Ecclesiastes 4:9-12 (King James Version KJV)

Chapter 4:
Perception of Marriage

We have discussed how perceptions of marriage come from what we have seen from our parents, the family we grew up in, or our role models. Our challenge, then, is to know whether our perception of marriage is right or wrong.

Removing the Blinders

As mentioned previously, most of our perceptions about life, marriage, and self, come from childhood experiences and may be a reflection of what our parents have or had. If we don't like our parents' relationship, we tell ourselves that we will not end up like them. But most often, we do.

The fact is, we prefer what we are used to, and that is why if we grew up with alcoholism, we may be drawn to an alcoholic. We might be drawn to an abuser. We might be drawn to the polar opposite of a Godly spouse. You see, everyone prefers their own mess.

A good illustration is how "at home" we are in our own bathrooms, even when it's a mess and our hair is all over the place. We have "clutter blindness" when it comes to our own bathrooms. But if we have to use the bathroom in another home, all the sudden the blinders come off! We avoid touching any surface, no matter how clean. Women may drive a hundred extra miles to their house rather than using a public restroom. That is how much we are used to our own mess.

Likewise, we are accustomed to what we know about marriage. We are comfortable with that standard, regardless of how awful it may be. And we are resistant to other outlooks and other examples, because they are unfamiliar. But the truth is, our marriages can (and often should) be different than our preconceived notions.

Changing Our Perceptions

As you read this, let me ask what perception of marriage you have:Is it based on your parents' example? Is it based on a romance novel in which a powerful, rich man falls in love with a poor, attractive woman and they lived happily ever after? Or is it based on "Soap Operas" such as The Young and the Restless, The Bold and Beautiful, and All My Children, where everyone has been married to everybody and sometimes three or four times over?

I challenge you today to look deep down and re-evaluate what you have perceived about marriage. As stated earlier, marriage is authored and instituted by God. Your perception of marriage should be anchored in what the Bible says is true. Now is the time to explore the scriptures and find the truth so that you can "tweak" your world- view.

In our era of information overload and overflow, things have become so relative that we get lost in the hype. We apply pseudo-science and the "talking-head" lingo we hear on television and social media. We take what we like and do away with what we don't; treating values as though they are disposable. Then we discover, too late, that our feelings and emotions are an inaccurate guide.

However, as Christians we can adopt our values from one reliable and unshakable source. If we believe that "In the beginning, God created the heavens and the earth," we should believe the rest. It is a terrible temptation to apply the "convenient" parts of the Bible and ignore the parts that require faith and obedience. But that temptation must be met head-on. We must embrace the whole truth in order to receive the blessings of a successful marriage.

An Analogy

Toyota, for instance, makes different models of cars, like sedans and trucks. For each vehicle produced, there is an owner's manual. What if a car mechanic used parts meant for a Prius to service a Forerunner or Sequoia? That car will not run smoothly, if at all. Why, then, would you use worldly principles, which are under the control of Satan, to start a divine institution ordained by God?

Do you know that Satan hates marriage, itself, because it is an ordinance of God? In fact, if your marriage glorifies God or enhances your gifts for use in the kingdom, you qualify for extra attacks. So as you read this, my question again is what is your perception of marriage? And where did you get it from?

Unintentional Toe-Stepping

In some instances, where mothers are the most dominant character in the home, their daughters will likely have the same character traits. Boys who grow up in this home will likely have more laid-back attitudes, like their fathers, as they grow up. This will not be a problem if a woman is attracted to a man like her father, or a man is attracted to a strong woman like his mother. Familiarity decreases the chance of future problems.

The problem comes, though, when a lady from the above scenario gets married to a man who comes from a home where the father is the dominant figure. If the man has learned to be like his father, then without meaning any harm the lady will step on his toes, and vice-versa. She will assume the role her mom played in her family- doing what comes naturally to her. But her actions will be met with resistance and defiance from a man who thinks, "She wants to dominate me." This lady may be surprised by this man's resistance and may even be confused, as she is doing her best with the finest intentions. The issue here may not always be personality, but perception of marriage and the roles each person plays within the union.

If the couple has a biblical perception of their roles, they will quickly resolve their issues amicably. If they prepare before they marry, they will identify their strengths and weaknesses with eyes wide open. They will understand each other's personalities and "get" what makes each "tick." This means they will be able to accept each other just as they are, but also work diligently to please the other party. They will trust the scriptures, give way gracefully, and build upon their strengths. This "give- and-take" is the highest form of respect, and is also the saving grace when two strong headed people tie the knot.

But what if these same two people ignore the scriptures, and instead, take their problems to a third party, namely moms or aunts? The problem may last for an extended period of time, because the mother of the wife will support her daughter, while the father of the husband will support his son. There will be a bigger rift as suspicion swirls on both sides. If care is not taken, this problem might be settled in the court, with the immediate parties thinking, "I thought she loved me" or "I thought he loved me."

The problem here may not be love, but wrong perceptions of marriage. Then again, each will be thinking, "If he/she loves me, then he/she will give in to my way." It is good to clear the air before the knot is tied.

The Best "Air Clearer"

Mutual respect is a great principle in marriage. Respecting one another (giving and taking) clears the air. It boils down to an understanding of roles… yes, good old fashioned roles. Male and female roles. Family roles that create harmony, unity, and ensure that everyone is on a trajectory of success.

Some might scream: "This is antiquated and misogynistic!" Some might protest for equal rights. Some might jump on the band-wagon and shop at gender-neutral stores like Target, which has removed its "boy toys" and "girl toys" labels. It seems like the world is trying to strip men and women of their God-given roles and purpose. This is ridiculous, because males should rejoice in their gender, and women should rejoice in their gender. It's okay to be male and female. It's okay to fulfill the precise roles God created us for.

Consider the love God has for us and his wonderful plan for our lives. He has provided a manual that brings peace, order and harmony to families. 1 Corinthians 13 defines "The Way of Love."

1 If I speak in the tongues of men and of angels, but have not love, I am a noisy gong or a clanging cymbal. 2 And if I have prophetic powers, and understand all mysteries and all knowledge, and if I have all faith, so as to remove mountains, but have not love, I am nothing. 3 If I give away all I have, and if I deliver up my body to be burned, but have not love, I gain nothing.

4 Love is patient and kind; love does not envy or boast; it is not arrogant 5 or rude. It does not insist on its own way; it is not irritable or resentful; 6 it does not rejoice at wrongdoing, but rejoices with the truth. 7 Love bears all things, believes all things, hopes all things, endures all things.

8 Love never ends. As for prophecies, they will pass away; as for tongues, they will cease; as for knowledge, it will pass away. 9 For we know in part and we prophesy in part, 10 but when the perfect comes, the partial will pass away. 11 When I was a child, I spoke like a child, I thought like a child, I reasoned like a child. When I became a man, I gave up childish ways. 12 For now we see in a mirror dimly, but then face to face. Now I know in part; then I shall know fully, even as I have been fully known.

13 So now faith, hope, and love abide, these three; but the greatest of these is love.

Aren't the scriptures beautiful? While God has ordained that man is the head of the household, this does not mean the woman has no-say in the order of things. This does not imply that a woman is less important or valued or powerful. It simply means that there are roles that can only be filled by a woman, just as there are roles that are ideally filled by a man. Men and women were made for each other, and are bound together by a powerful love that transcends gender.

After all, a wife is the neck that supports the head. If the neck hurts, the head cannot move freely. If the neck is stuck, the head is stuck also. If there is a head injury, the whole body falters. If there is a break in the neck bones, the rest of the body is paralyzed. So using the Bible as a tool to dominate or inflate an ego is folly. Rather, God shows us that we are to celebrate the strengths that each party brings to a marriage. The mission is to elevate and enhance the positives and "pull on the same rope" — just as our ancestors did. In doing so, husbands and wives are able to give each other what they need… in abundance.

See? Old-fashioned works- if you understand the root concept and celebrate our God-given differences!

Think about it.

Mutual respect is a great principle in marriage. Respecting one another (giving and taking) clears the air.

Chapter 5:
Who We Are

Again, we are not animals. We did not evolve out of slime or a burst of cosmic dust. We are fearfully and wonderfully made by God, who knit our bones in our mothers' wombs. We were created in His image for a purpose. And we were created male and female for a reason.

As a child of God, you should know that human beings are spirits with souls that live in a body. In other words, we are:

1. Spirit
2. Soul
3. Body

Connecting the Dots

Body. Let's start with the body first. You may be attracted to somebody in the physical, and that is how many relationships start. But our bodies crumble, age and become wrinkled. If our marriage is solely based on physical attributes, then our union will diminish over time as our bodies diminish. It's like a seed that is sown on shallow ground. There is no nourishment from the earth below. It cannot thrive or produce any fruit.

Soul level. Physical attraction should be a precursor to a soul level connection. Connecting with someone at the soul level is far deeper than just physical attraction. You may have heard of someone saying, "She/he is my soul mate!" But the soul- level isn't the end-all and be-all of a relationship. In fact, the soul level is where emotions and reasoning reign. Emotions can be good and bad. Emotions can be affected by external circumstances. Some decisions made at this level are dependent on how we feel at any given moment. Feelings, alone, are not enough for marriage survival.

Spiritual level. When you are connected to somebody at a spiritual level, it is considered the deepest level of communication. If the Spirit of God resides in you, as well as in the other person, there is oneness of purpose and unity. The spirit is fixed and anchored, more-so than the soul. Therefore, the relationship is much more dependable at this level. As a child of God, the spirit of God resides in you. Never, ever join in a relationship with someone who has suppressed the voice of the Spirit within.

Perfecting your Perception

As you are waiting on the Lord to meet your spouse, this is an excellent time to think of your own perception of marriage and compare it to what God shares in His book. Connect the body-soul-spirit dots so that you can discern the difference. Understand the wonderful, edifying God-given roles each gender has been assigned. What an honor it is to be male or female, knowing that God created us specifically for a great mission — marriage.

Think about It.

As you wait on the Lord to meet your spouse, this is an excellent time to think of your own perception of marriage and compare it to what God shares in his book.

Chapter 6:
Know Yourself

If somebody asks who you are, the most natural answer would be, "I am Mr. /Ms. So-and-So" or "I am the daughter/son to Mr. /Ms. ABC." Some other answers could be, "I am a teacher, doctor, nurse, Realtor, social worker, lawyer, mother, or father." But if you were instructed not to write your name, occupation, relationship, or marital status, how would you describe yourself? What does that little voice in your head constantly say about "you?" That is the core of what you believe about yourself. Sometimes it is inaccurate, and sometimes it is vague. And most of the time, it needs "tweaked" before you begin to contemplate marriage.

Our world is so noisy that we hardly have moments of quietness to search our souls and spirits and get to know ourselves. It is easier to study other people and understand them, which means we neglect self-exploration. How much of yourself do you really know? It's time to get acquainted with who you really are.

Case in Point

Years ago, I had a patient who had a kidney problem. She had not surrendered her life to Christ, but was a very good person. Her sister was a believer in Christ, and I prayed with her in agreement that God would give her sister a brand new kidney. As we said "Amen," my patient said, "I don't want a new kidney. I want mine because that is also me."

Her sister and I were taken aback as she canceled our prayer.

Sadly, my patient didn't understand that she is a spirit with a soul, and that she lives in a human body. A new kidney would not change who she really is — a spirit with a soul — but would simply help make her human body function. As a unbeliever, she had no clue.

Self-Study

I want to assure you that no one has a perfect life. Perhaps we look up to people who seems to have it all, but realistically they probably feel about themselves the way the rest of us feel. The only difference is that they have learned to cover their feelings well. They are able to hide their insecurities and imperfections, but are a work in progress, just as we all are.

We are all on a journey, and the point is to learn about ourselves. This allows us to change our perceptions of marriage and relationships. It forces us to ask, "How much do I truly know about me?" and "What is my philosophy about life?" and "What are my life goals?"

It helps to answer the following questions:

- ❖ How do I resolve conflict?
- ❖ What is my personality type?
- ❖ What are my strengths?
- ❖ How do I learn, by reading, writing, or listening?
- ❖ What are my weaknesses?
- ❖ Who are my friends?
- ❖ Who am I a friend to?
- ❖ Am I really who people think I am?
- ❖ Who do I confide in?
- ❖ Am I trustworthy?
- ❖ Have I shown honor and respect to those who deserve them in my life?

- ❖ What is my purpose in life?
- ❖ What goals do I have to achieve my purpose?
- ❖ Who are my heroes?
- ❖ Who are my mentors?
- ❖ Have I developed my mind in the past year?
- ❖ Am I a dream helper or dream killer?
- ❖ What do I actually want in a spouse?
- ❖ What is my view of life?
- ❖ What is the point of reference for my every decision?

How God Sees You

Why is it important that we know ourselves better? If I don't know "me" how can I expect another person who was raised in another family, by different parents, with his individual set of world views, to know or understand me? If I don't know my personal strengths, how can I use them to help someone else? If I don't know my own weaknesses, how can I allow another person to help me work on them to improve myself?

Who are you really? Alternatively, who do you think you are? Have you allowed anyone to define you contrary to what your heavenly Father says you are? Who we are as children of God has nothing to do with our physical, mental, material, and societal attributes. It has everything to do with the finished work of Christ and what our Father in heaven calls us.

When we see ourselves as mortal beings, then any flaw in our fleshly nature becomes a big issue. When we see ourselves through the eyes of others, we may feel "less than." But when we see ourselves through the lens of salvation, then our flaws, peeves, and idiosyncrasies suddenly diminish. We can lay them at the foot of the cross. We are no longer defined by our failures, but are defined by the divine. It encourages us to follow Christ's example and live by the Golden Rule, especially in our marriages: "Do unto others as you would have them do unto you."

Biblical Examples

In David, people saw a shepherd boy, but God saw a king. Paul (when he was Saul) persecuted Christians, but God told Ananias that he had chosen Paul to carry the Gospel of Christ to the gentiles. The world saw Sarah as a ninety-year-old barren woman, but God made her the mother of many nations.

Who are you seeing? Who are the people around you seeing in you that you have erroneously believed contrary to what God sees in you?

Do the Work

God says you are a prince or a princess. You are blood-washed, even though the accuser tries to undermine you daily. The "father of all lies" reminds you of all the times you missed the mark. But your Maker says you are a royal priest, a saint, blessed and highly favored, seated in heavenly places above principalities and powers. You may not see yourself as that currently, but it is still the truth. This is why it is important for you to take time to know yourself — certainly before you meet your future spouse. Know who you really are. By doing so, you are preparing yourself for your mate.

Do the work. You will have better insight about who you are, and this will lead you to examine how you "treat yourself." If you are always cutting yourself down, you can adjust your attitude. If you think too highly of yourself, you can adjust your attitude. Our "self-image" and how we perceive our identities comes from our earlier interactions with our families, peers, and others who have left an impression on our subconscious minds. But we are not slaves to the past. In fact, we are masters of the future… because God has a plan for us. Knowing ourselves and embracing our identity in Christ helps us keep a healthy self-image.

Self-Esteem (Not Self-Conceit) Brings Balance

Of course, self-esteem due to who we are in Christ is totally different from self-conceit. When you know your worth and who you are, you won't underestimate yourself in marriage.

You insult your heavenly Father when you persist in having

negative images about yourself. In fact, negativity attracts negativity; meaning you risk attracting a spouse who will treat you badly. If you don't think you deserve better, you will settle for anyone, even when it is obviously a bad choice. You will tell yourself that this may be your last chance. Not only that, but your attitude will transmit to prospective in-laws, who will perceive you just as you think you deserve to be treated.

On the other end of the spectrum are those who think too highly of themselves. Be careful, as the Bible says that one of the things that God hates the most is pride. There is a saying that goes, "Conceit is a weird disease. It makes everybody sick except the one who has it." It is always better to refer to your Maker who knew you and created a path for you before time began. Jeremiah 1:5 says, "Before I formed you in the womb, I knew you, before you were born, I set you apart; I appointed you as a prophet to the nations."

You need to get a clear definition of who you are and what God has made you to be. It is important to get this concept from your Maker as other sources may be contaminated due to the sin-nature of man, different world views, and different experiences. Thus, if I am docile and quiet, Mr./Ms. B will think I am a wonderful person. At the same time, it will make me repulsive to Mr./Ms. A, who wants a loud and outgoing person. If I view myself from the eyes of these two people, I will be conflicted. If I see myself through God's eyes, then it is perfect because He knows me better than anyone else.

Our world is so noisy that we hardly have moments of quietness to search our souls and spirits and get to know ourselves. It is easier to study other people and understand them, which means we neglect self-exploration.

Chapter 7:
What Does the Bible Say You Are?

According to God's word, you are an express image of Jehovah God on earth, Genesis (1V 27): Made a little lower than an angel; (Heb, 2 V 7); Crowned with glory and honor; (Psalm 8 Vs 3-5); You are seated with Christ in heavenly places, Ephesians 2 V 6. You are a dwelling place of the Holy Spirit, (1 Corinthians 3 V 16). You have been empowered to trample upon serpents and scorpions and every power of the enemy, (Luke 10 V 19). You are blood-washed (Rev 7 V 14), and ransomed from the power of death and hell, (Hosea, 13 V 14). You have power to bind and lose, (Mathew, 18 V 18). God has made you, yes you, the fear and dread of God against the kingdom of darkness; a member of the body of Christ (1 Corinthians 12:12-27); an heir of God, and a joint heir with Christ, (Romans 8 V 17).

Trust God's Opinion Above All Others

Since the word of God confirms that we are everything mentioned above, why would we let ourselves (or anyone else, for that matter) tell us otherwise? Now that you and I know better, why don't we start living in the reality of what and who God has made us to be in Christ Jesus.

Inside of you is a wealth of untapped potentials, incredible possibilities and capabilities. You may be a rough-cut diamond, but a rare gem anyway. You are very special to God who has made you for his own glory. You may not realize it because you have been operating at a shallow level that is in the physical realm. Now that you are connected to the Spirit of God, He will begin to show you those things that have been laid down in your spirit. All these have been said to say, do not let anyone—even you—make you feel less than who God has created you to be.

Most importantly, do not let your mind do you in. The way you feel about you makes you react to others. I would like to ask you again: "who are you" Have you known yourself any better than you did prior to reading this chapter? Why is this issue very important?

A Prayer

One of the problems most singles experience is feeling that something is wrong with them. Maybe that is why they are still single, especially if it is not by choice. The fact of the matter is, nothing is wrong with you! In most cases, God has a better plan for you. Allow me to pray for you.

Father in heaven, I pray for the dear ones reading this chapter. I pray that You will help these individuals realize who you have made them to be by your Spirit, and not by what people have told them — not the lies the Enemy has told them, not what they have told themselves, but that your Spirit would let these individuals know who You have made them to be. Let them begin today to function in that knowledge in order that their lives would bring you glory. As they begin to know themselves, let your favor come over them. Let your joy be their strength. Father, please clear away every cloud of heaviness that is hanging over their spirits. Let their spirits arise from deep within and praise your holy name. In Jesus' name I pray. Amen.

All that good stuff happens when you receive Jesus as your Lord and Savior. You may ask me what that means. It means that every man is a sinner. You and I included. We all deserve to die, as it is written, "The soul that sinned shall die" (Ezekiel 18:20).

Defining the Enemy

Sin came into the world due to rebellion. Lucifer, the most beautiful being ever made, strayed from the presence of God when he decided to take the glory that was due God. He was thrown out of Heaven, along with some angels, to earth. He hates

God, but since he cannot do anything to God, he attacks the creation that God loves the most: man. Satan's desire is to take as many to hell as possible so they would spend eternity with him instead of with God in Heaven.

We see Satanic attacks all over the world, but the most insidious are those Satan launches against families. He tries his utmost to weaken families through immorality, relativism, trash on the television, and through the influence of high profile nonbelievers. At times, our own homes are a portal through which we invite evil. Think about it. When we listen to raunchy music, watch disgraceful shows, and dress like shameless celebrities... then we are imitating evil and inviting it into our midst.

Instead, we should invite God's best into our lives and saturate our homes with his glory, goodness, mercy, and power. Why not listen to and support Christian radio? How about listening to some absolutely wonderful contemporary Christian CDs? Gospel music? Sermons? How about Googling the old fashioned values upon which our nation was built? Why not study the successful marriages of yesteryears — the Internet is filled with uplifting quotes from men and women who have experienced it firsthand!

The Bible on Marriage

We can all use some inspiration when learning more about the institution of marriage. The Bible, of course, is the most trusted foundation for study. The scriptures below describe God's wishes regarding this special union:

- ❖ Genesis 2:22 ~22 "Then the LORD God made a woman from the rib he had taken out of the man, and he brought her to the man. 23 The man said, "This is now bone of my bones and flesh of my flesh; she shall be called 'woman, ' for she was taken out of man. 24 For this reason a man will leave his father and mother and be united to his wife, and they will become one flesh."

- ❖ Proverbs 18:22 ~22 "He who finds a wife finds what is good and receives favor from the LORD."

- ❖ Proverbs 19:14 ~14 "Houses and wealth are inherited from parents, but a prudent wife is from the LORD."
- ❖ Ephesians 5:22-23 ~22 Wives, submit to your husbands as to the Lord. 23 For the husband is the head of the wife as Christ is the head of the church, his body, of which he is the Savior. 24 Now as the church submits to Christ, so also wives should submit to their husbands in everything. 25 Husbands, love your wives, just as Christ loved the church and gave himself up for her 26 to make her holy, cleansing her by the washing with water through the word, 27 and to present her to himself as a radiant church, without stain or wrinkle or any other blemish, but holy and blameless. 28 In this same way, husbands ought to love their wives as their own bodies. He who loves his wife loves himself. 29 After all, no one ever hated his own body, but he feeds and cares for it, just as Christ does the church— 30 for we are members of his body. 31 For this reason a man will leave his father and mother and be united to his wife, and the two will become one flesh. 32 This is a profound mystery—but I am talking about Christ and the church. 33 However, each one of you also must love his wife as he loves himself, and the wife must respect her husband ~
- ❖ Matthew 19:4-6 ~ 4 "Haven't you read," he replied, "that at the beginning the Creator 'made them male and female,' 5 and said, 'For this reason a man will leave his father and mother and be united to his wife, and the two will become one flesh' ? 6 So they are no longer two, but one. Therefore what God has joined together, let man not separate."

What people said about Marriage

- ❖ "Let the wife make the husband glad to come home, and let him make her sorry to see him leave." ~ Martin Luther
- ❖ "I hold an old-fashioned notion that a happy marriage is the crown of a woman's life." ~ Beatrix Potter
- ❖ "Marriage was ordained for a remedy and to increase the world and for the man to help the woman and the woman the man, with all love and kindness." ~ William Tyndale
- ❖ "Love seems the swiftest but is the slowest of all growths. No man or woman really knows what perfect love is until

they have been married a quarter of a century." ~ Mark Twain

- ❖ "When a man of sense comes to marry, it is a companion whom he wants, and not an artist. It is not merely a creature who can paint, and play, and sing, and draw, and dress, and dance; it is a being who can comfort and counsel him; one who can reason and reflect, and feel, and judge, and discourse, and discriminate; one who can assist him in his affairs, lighten his cares, sooth his sorrows, strengthen his principles, and educate his children." ~ Hannah More

- ❖ "In marriage do thou be wise: prefer the person before money, virtue before beauty, the mind before the body; then thou hast a wife, a friend, a companion, a second self." ~ William Penn

- ❖ "The very crown of marriage is mutual delight and contentment." ~ C. H. Spurgeon

- ❖ "Come, let's be a comfortable couple and take care of each other! How glad we shall be, that we have somebody we are fond of always, to talk to and sit with." ~ Charles Dickens

- ❖ "The highest happiness on earth is marriage." ~ William Lyon Phelps

- ❖ "The sum which two married people owe to one another defies calculation. It is an infinite debt, which can only be discharged through eternity." ~ Johann Wolfgang von Goethe

- ❖ "What a happy and holy fashion it is that those who love one another should rest on the same pillow." ~ Nathaniel Hawthorne

Accepting the Greatest Gift

Have you noticed that you don't have to teach children to misbehave? They already know how to misbehave. It's ingrained in our fallen nature, which is why it is so important to choose a Godly spouse. Together you can teach children to be all that God has called them to be… not that any of us will ever be perfect. But we can encourage our children to follow God's path from the cradle to the grave, while positively shaping their perception of who they are. How wonderful when children see a Christian dynamic in their parent's marriage! This is made possible through Jesus' sacrifice and example.

Thankfully, God's great, merciful, and generous feat was to redeem mankind from the eternal damnation by sending Jesus to die on the cross. The truth is that we deserve to die shamefully, but God chose Jesus to die in our place. The blood He shed on the cross paid the penalty for our sins. The price has been paid, but we are required to come forward and accept it into our lives. Only then is it effective. Only then does the Spirit of God begin to release all the hidden things He laid deep within us. Have you ever accepted Jesus as Lord in your life?

Let me illustrate this simple fact with an example of someone who is left millions as an inheritance. He doesn't know, so he lives like a pauper, homeless, even though he is a millionaire. Unless he goes to court and presents evidence that says who he says he is, he will not claim his inheritance and will not be able to spend that money. He will remain poor through ignorance, even though he is rich. However, if he shows himself and claims his estate, he can spend that money.

How many in the world are potential "spiritual millionaires," but don't know it! The sacrifice has been paid, but we need to claim it in order to enjoy God's abundant blessings. It is simple. Acknowledge that you are a sinner; confess all your sins to God. Ask God to forgive you, to cleanse you with the blood of Jesus, and ask Jesus to come into your life and be the Lord of your life. That is all.

There is no perfect individual, so whoever we allow to define us comes with his or her flaws, peeves, and idiosyncrasies. When we define ourselves, we bring our own issues; however, when we see ourselves from the eyes of the one who put us together, we get a much better view of ourselves.

Chapter 8:
New in Christ

Romans 10:9–10 says, "With the heart, you believe and with your mouth, confession is made unto righteousness." You are now a brand-new creature in Christ. Old things have passed away, and all things have become new. Welcome to the family of God!

Whatever you genuinely confessed and repented of before God is forgiven. You must determine not to sin again, but this does not mean you will not make mistakes. You will, but you will also recognize it and confess it to God. Then you can move ahead.

Preparing Ourselves for Marriage

Now that you are beginning to know yourself better, you may wonder why you see yourself the way you do. Why do you think the way you think? As mentioned in prior chapters, your self-perception is linked to childhood experiences and learned behaviors. It is time to challenge the paradigm you have developed over the years.

An important step is to admit the need for change. First, we must realize there is a problem. The way we see that problem is equally important. For instance, what some may call a problem, others may see as a challenge. Those who see it as a big problem may retreat into their shells like a snail and remain there. Those who perceive the same issue as an obstacle to achieving a set goal will do everything humanly possible to forge ahead. In fact, they are determined to defeat the roadblock even if it means climbing over, going around, digging underneath, or tunneling through it. Which one of these two people are you? Do you give up when things don't drop into your lap, or do you push forward?

Another area where knowing makes a difference is in handling criticism. This is one area we all have to deal with, because (one way or another) we are going to be criticized — justly and unjustly. Knowing how to handle it is important, especially when contemplating marriage. Maturity is recognizing when to take a criticism seriously, learn from it, and become even better from it. Putting up a wall at each criticism may rob us of the chance to do better. Constant criticism on the other hand may make us feel less than smart if everything we do is wrong, especially coming from those close to us. If our closest friends and family members feel badly about themselves, one way to feel better is to put other people down. We also have to recognize this.

You are now at a certain stage in your journey toward self-awareness. It's time to learn how to make others understand when to stop criticizing you unjustly. Learn this now so that you can truly be ready for a spouse. One preacher suggested having one "enemy" on your team so you will constantly be up and doing instead of having everyone around you as your cheerleader. He meant that everyone needs someone who will tell it as it is… someone who loves us enough to tell us the truth (or at least their version of the truth). How do you handle the truth? Are you able to discern when the criticism comes out of love, jealousy, or hatred?

Assessing Your Decisions

As we get to know ourselves better, the next issue is defining the decision-making yardstick. How do you arrive at your decisions? When you look at the last ten major decisions you have made, on a scale of one being the worst and one hundred being the best, how would you rate yourself? Would you say 50 percent or less, or 100 percent satisfaction?

The fact is, some of our decisions are made on a whim… and then consequences come. We ponder, "What was I thinking?" If we do not make conscious efforts to learn from these mistakes, we will most likely repeat the same mistakes in the future. Therefore, it makes sense to keep track of the decisions we have made (and will make) in life. We should note the reasons for our decisions and the anticipated outcomes, then come back in three months, six months, nine months, or a year, and see how those have panned out. This will allow us to pinpoint what decision-making processes worked, and what didn't.

Now let's apply our decision-making to choosing a life partner. What points are we considering? More importantly, where and how did we go wrong in our last relationship? We should be able to pinpoint what went wrong so that the history will not repeat itself. If we have used the same yardstick and made two serious decisions and did not get the projected outcomes, then we have to think twice before doing so again. You have to get back to the drawing table and see what the problem was.

Creatures of Habit

Your daily routines and habits matter. They determine what your life will culminate to at the end of the day. The time you use is, basically, your "life," so don't waste it (we'll look more closely at this in the next chapter).

Our daily habits can make us or break us. What is a habit? Webster has several definitions, ranging from clothing to mental and physiological aspects. For this discourse, we will use four:

- ❖ Manner of conducting oneself (bearing)
- ❖ Prevailing disposition or character of a person's thoughts and feelings (mental makeup)
- ❖ A settled tendency or usual manner of behavior (taking daily walks)
- ❖ A behavior pattern acquired by frequent repetition or physiologic exposure that shows itself in regularity or increased facility of performance.

Every definition connotes something that is repeatedly done and becomes involuntary. Whether it is going to bed late, waking up early, eating junk, or drinking alcohol, a habit is very difficult to break. If we are doing the identical thing every day, we will definitely have a duplicate result. In fact, it is madness if we continually do the same thing and expect a different result.

Are you habitually wasting time, making wrong decisions, or gravitating toward harmful relationships? If so, it is time for a paradigm shift. Remember, you are new in Christ. You are a new being, which means old habits can fall away. In their place come new healthy habits that edify our bodies, souls and spirits. Again, we should see ourselves the way God sees us. So the most important shift we can make is what we think of ourselves — and making sure our self-perceptions are right. Knowing why we think the way we do is the solution. It changes lives for the better, because we can correct faulty perceptions and be all God has called us to be.

If we think correctly as a matter of habit, then we know we are not accidents. We know we are not mistakes. We know we were born for a reason and can start living in a purposeful manner. We can wake up each day thinking, "Where can I cause a change today?" It does not mean we will not have ups and downs, but we will realize the ups and downs are building blocks that will make our lives better, our faith stronger, and our successes all the sweeter.

According to Proverbs 23:7, "As a man thinketh in his heart, so is he" (KJV). What are you habitually thinking? Like they say, do you see the glass as half full or half empty? Do you always see yourself as a victim or a victor, healthy or sick, prosperous or a failure, the head or the tail? Since negative ways of thinking have not been productive for you in the past, what do you have to lose by going in the opposite direction?

Healthy Change

Changing your thought pattern can be done, but you must be totally involved. Those in the medical field will tell you that the human body does not permit a vacuum. Each time a vacuum is created it is likely to be filled with fluid. Therefore you have to displace negative mindset and thought patterns with something more powerful than your habits.

So what is more powerful than your habits? The scriptures, of course! Keep track of your thoughts, and when you notice pessimism creeping in, stop for a moment and ask yourself, "Where did that come from?

Think about it.

Are you habitually wasting time, making wrong decisions, or gravitating toward harmful relationships? If so, it is time for a paradigm shift.

Chapter 9:
Changing Paradigms

What is a paradigm? It is a typical example, pattern or model of something. The way we see ourselves results from the way we think — a paradigm. Then, the ways we think make us act and react in certain ways. When we habitually act that way, it becomes our way of life and seals our destiny. Yes, our way of thinking can make us or break us. Our thinking is a result of how we have been conditioned to think.

Stinkin' Thinkin'

If while growing up, we heard, "You can't do this or that," we end up believing that lie. If, on the other hand, we have been conditioned to think nothing is impossible, we are inclined to do our very best without sabotaging ourselves with negative thinking.

To usher in permanent changes means we must challenge the authenticity of paradigms that have shaped our lives. Again, we go back to childhood experiences. If we have suffered from any form of abuse in childhood—physical, mental, sexual, or whatever—this causes us to have guilt. As children, our coping mechanism was to bury those harrowing (and guilt-riddled) memories in our subconscious minds and forget it.

However, guilt brings shame, and both are very painful and unforgiving emotions. Much as we try to suppress them, they usually show up in other areas of our lives. Once in a while they bubble up to the surface, and we act out. Most importantly, it makes us think we are bad and undeserving. We become doormats to others just because of that singular act.

Stopping the Cycle

No matter how deep we bury our childhood experiences, they consistently control our lives. Sexual abuse often leads to promiscuity, which brings further guilt and shame. If you have been sexually active, become pregnant, and had an abortion, the guilt and self-blame can be overwhelming. You may overcome it, settle down and start a family, but deep down inside, you are not healed. Your subconscious feelings of being a second class citizen can be passed to your children, who learn from you.

To break the cycle and ensure the next generation has a healthy self-perception, talk to a counselor or mature Christian. That's the first step in healing, especially if you have suffered sexual abuse or rape in the past. It is very important that you confront that issue in your life. The good news is that the Bible says, "Do not conform to the pattern of this world, but be transformed by the renewing of your mind. Then you will be able to test and approve what God's will is—his good, pleasing and perfect will of God" (Romans 12:2).

Taking Responsibility

This puts the burden of correction of negative thinking back on you and me. No, it is not easy being honest with yourself. It is not easy changing the paradigms in your life. But consider this: if you are going for a job interview and think to yourself, "They may not hire me because of this and that," the interviewer may not hire you. We may rationalize to ourselves that our negative thoughts cushion us from rejection. But no, that is not correct. You helped the person decide not to give you the job because your actions followed your thoughts.

Some executives have chosen less-qualified candidates over those who are better qualified just because of their personalities. Those people went out thinking, "I may not be the best candidate, but I will do everything in my power to impress the panel."

Are we now discussing job interviews in a marriage preparation book? No, but someone who says, "I know they will not hire me," may also think, "They will not ask me out a second time because nobody does." Put yourself in this person's shoes. Who is supposed to ask you out a second time if all he/she has heard from you is how everything you touch goes south instead of north? Why wouldn't this person think, "Is he/she going to take me south too?

The Battle is in Your Mind

Every person wants upward mobility in life and needs a partner who will help accelerate that upward move. Just think about it— imagine meeting someone at 9:00 p.m. for the first time. He says to you, "Someone I used to see has been trying to embarrass me by showing up each time I go out on a date. This person has anger management issues and gets violent sometimes. This individual has been out of town but will be back tomorrow." Then he turns around and says, "Can we go out tomorrow?" Are you going to say yes to this person? Maybe you are adventurous or want to be on the evening news. I am not that adventurous, and I will not go out with this person till he has sorted himself out.

Maybe you don't have an ex who is harassing the daylights out of you, but you have painted a picture of yourself on this first date that says, "I am the Dead Sea. Nothing in me works." We know that is not true, because every individual has his or her strengths and weaknesses. You may not have discovered your strengths yet, but rather have focused on your weaknesses. Continuously thinking that way leads to a pattern, which eventually becomes a stronghold.

The battle is in your mind. The Bible takes time to explain this in Ephesians 6:10–12 that says

Finally, be strong in the Lord and in the strength of His might. Put on the full armor of God, so that you will be able to stand firm against the schemes of the devil, for our struggle is not against flesh and blood, but against the rulers, against the authorities, against the powers of this dark world and against the spiritual forces of evil in the heavenly realms.

Beware Of the Father of All Lies

The Devil — the father of all lies — puts those thoughts, suggestions, and negative images in our mind. He makes it look like you are the one thinking them. Then you begin to believe the lies and will always have reasons to justify them.

But the Word of God gives us a solution in 2 Corinthians 10:5:

"We demolish arguments and every pretension that sets itself up against the knowledge of God, and we take captive every thought to make it obedient to Christ" (NIV). The Aramaic Bible in Plain English states it this way: "And we pull down reasoning's and every high thing that is exalted against the knowledge of God, and we take all minds prisoner to the obedience of The Messiah." Have you subjected your mind under the authority of Christ? When you do, you will only see yourself as Christ sees you and nothing less. You will begin to demolish every other argument that runs contrary to what Christ says about you. Take that, Devil!

Listen to Colossians 2:14–15:

"Having canceled the charge of our legal indebtedness, which stood against us and condemned us; he has taken it away, nailing it to the cross. And having disarmed the powers and authorities, he made a public spectacle of them, triumphing over them by the cross."

Now read Romans 8:1:

"Therefore there is now no condemnation for those who are in Christ Jesus" (NIV).

If you have truly repented of your sins, do not let the enemy of your soul keep you from your entitlement as a child of God by reminding you constantly of what has been finished. Deal with this issue head-on and you will understand that you don't have a problem; but that those who did it to you are sick. This will free you to know that you are valuable and you deserve better. How, you may ask? Truly acknowledge your sins, confess them to God, and repent. Resolve never to do them again, and ask the Holy Spirit to help you. The Bible says, "As far as the east is from the west so has he removed our transgression from us" (Ps. 103:12). In 1 John 1:9 it is written, "If we confess our sins, he is faithful and just to forgive us."

A Clear View of Consequences

Another decision making "must" is having a clear view of all the possible consequences that could result. The better informed you are, the more you can decide what is beneficial. Some very successful people have mastered how they make decisions and also noted what influenced them when they made the biggest decisions that paid off.

As Christians, we have to rely on the leading of the Holy Spirit to make decisions that will best represent God's will for our lives. Some call it intuition, others a sixth sense. Others call it "something." Whatever you call it, if you can learn to be sensitive to the Holy Sprit's leading and direction in your life, you will have much fewer headaches — and negative consequences. "The blessings of the Lord make one rich, He does not add any sorrow to it" (Proverbs 10:22). If you have God's perfect will in everything, your life will be more peaceful and quieter than most.

Now, if eight out of ten decisions you made in the last three months did not turn out right, you need to check your method. If the opposite is the case, then you know you are on the right track. When we base our reasons on emotion, we should expect some problems. But we can never go wrong when we are led by the Holy Spirit. Likewise, when we base our reasons for choosing a partner on physical attributes alone, we should accept what comes with it.

Be Careful What You Wish For

Here's an analogy. An African man living in America in the '90s asked his relatives back home to help him get a spouse. His qualifications were that she must be a nurse, tall, slim, and light in complexion. Those were the things most important to this shallow fellow, who would probably not make a good companion to a lady with high intellectual prowess. He desired physical and fiscal qualities, much like women who want handsome and rich men. The problem is, a handsome, rich man could be an armed robber and a wife abuser. Get it? There has to be more substance to a lifetime relationship!

In short, be careful what you wish for. If your spouse tells you to have an affair with another man or woman so you can get a multimillion-dollar contract, what will you do? What if your fiancé suggests you work at a strip club to rack up quick money for your extravagant wedding? What if someone tells you to have an intimacy with his friend as a way of showing your love to him/her? Obviously, those who are fixated on the physical have short-changed themselves... and will short change you. These people are ignorant weaklings when it comes to soul and spirit. For those who are grounded in Christ, they serve as teachable moments — examples of choices NOT to make.

The fact is, God wants good for you, not evil. He has given you a body, soul. and spirit that is above and beyond adequate! You have the tools at your fingertips and can "tweak" your personal paradigm. In the following chapters we will take a closer look at what success means from God's perspective and how your definition of it can affect every area of your life, including marriage.

Think about it.

Every person, including you and I, want upward mobility in life and need a partner who will help accelerate that upward move.

Chapter 10:
Putting Your Life on Hold

Some ladies who are still waiting for "Mr. Right" tend to put their lives on hold. They don't bother about seeking higher degrees or investing in anything that would enhance their lives. Some do this because they are focused like a laser, on finding their mate, expending all their time and energy in that pursuit. Others feel that self-improvement is a waste of time, because their perfect mate would love them just as they are. Less self-confident women may think that men are threatened by a well-read lady.

The truth is, some men are threatened by a woman's level of success. It's much better to find that out beforehand than after the vows have been taken. What happens if you want to self-improve after the wedding? What if you find professional success after you are married? If your spouse discourages self-improvement, your marriage will be in trouble. Your husband may feel you are "showing off" or "showing him up." He may feel his sole role is to be breadwinner, which causes him to feel threatened, emasculated or, in the worst case, jealous. He may insist on standing at the upper rung of the ladder while you are waiting at the bottom.

Denying Your Future?

If you have the ability and the motivation to enhance yourself, but fail to act, you are denying your own future. If you do so to placate a spouse, then you will be frustrated. You may feel unfulfilled. Think of it this way: the Lord's timing is the best. Perhaps your spouse is out their waiting for you to become the well-rounded person God wants you to be. One thing for sure is the further you go in your career, education, or another area, the better you will be able to take care of yourself and your children if the Lord so blesses you.

I am not by any means suggesting that you chase a dream just for the sake of chasing a dream. All I am saying is that women should not neglect a higher degree just because it might intimidate a potential suitor. Rather, in most cases the opposite is the case when God is in it.

Even if you don't want to go to college, take up a hobby or involve yourself with a church group. This will help you stay busy and stave off some of the lonely times. The Enemy wants you to feel sorry for yourself. However, investing in the community brings joy and fulfillment that comes from blessing others. As a side benefit, staying active helps you avoid extra calories that you would have consumed being a couch potato. Even a trip to a local library will open up a world of books and places you didn't know existed. There are outdoor theaters, free open-air concerts that are family- friendly, and charitable events to support. Being active in your local church will keep you reasonably engaged. It's all about balance and the right motivation.

Taking Time for "You"

By the same token, you don't want to be so occupied that you can't have "quiet time." Remember, "In repentance and rest is your salvation, in quietness and trust is your strength, but you would have none of it." (Isa. 30:15). Find time to rest, reflect and pray. This, too, edifies the mind and body.

God made you, knows you, and has allowed you to go through experiences: some painful. He may have caused one or two relationships to end. Then, like Ruth and Esther, it may well be that he has prepared a spouse for you who is meant to find and complete you. The Bible says in Proverbs 18:22, "He who findeth a wife findeth a good thing and obtaineth favor from God." It didn't say she who finds a husband. There is an implication here that the woman will be found, and the man seeks. If you have been looking and you believe God, stop looking for a man and look to God, who can arrange any meeting, even in the most obscure places.

Blessings in Disguise

Sometimes the best things in life are found in hidden places. Sometimes we find a gem in the worst environments. Gold, diamonds, silver, copper, and oil are all buried deep in the belly of the earth. When they are brought up, they go through several processes before they become finished products. If you see them prior to purification, they may not look like they are worth much. But after purification, they are glorious.

It is much the same with human beings. Prayer and discernment can help you sort the "unpolished gems" from those who are simply lazy, unmotivated, or have bad character traits. If you refuse a God given, God chosen, brother or a sister before they become "perfect," you are turning down a potential match made in heaven. You see, women sometimes judge men who haven't yet made a commercial success of their lives. Perhaps these men are still trying to find themselves and are working toward a goal. Yet a judgmental woman might say, "I'm too good for this one." In many instances, this is their loss.

After all, human beings are "a work in progress". The sister who doesn't look a bit like Ms. America may be a butterfly hidden inside a cocoon. A brother who has hidden promises and blessings may simply be waiting for counsel to help attain his goals. In both cases, their circumstances may be blessings in disguise, just waiting for their intended spouses to polish them into brilliance. Seek the Lord's face and approval.

Lost Opportunity

This reminds me of a story; Several years ago, a man was dating a girl. What he did not know was that his friend had noticed all the sterling qualities in this lady and knew she was wife material. This man traveled abroad without committing to this lady. He met another lady and mentioned her to his friend, without any intention of a serious relationship with his new "love interest." In fact, his plan was to marry the girl he left behind when he was ready. That never happened because his friend used it as an opportunity to woo and marry the woman left behind. The irony is that the man did not recognize the gem in his hands, while his friend did. The friend married her within nine months after his friend left. Some friend, you might say!

I also would like to tell you a story of a lady I will call Mina. About thirty years ago she was living as a maid with a couple who took her overseas. She was in her twenties at the time and learned the language. Later she did secretarial studies. When she came back, a struggling man approached her for marriage. He was living in a one-room kitchen line building. This lady made such fun of him. However, after three months the man landed a big contract, bought a car, and moved into a three-bedroom flat. Mina, who told me this story, now wanted to go back to him. She said that the man asked her, "Are you trying to come around me just because of the car and the three bedrooms?"

Maybe it wasn't the will of God that she married this man, but I told this story to make a point. Tables turn. God can move one up and another down (Ps. 75:7). Do not automatically refuse someone because they seem "less than." Their lives can change for the better.

In other words, do not let financial gains be the sole reason you accept or refuse anyone. You could get someone who is successful financially today and is down the next. What will you do then? Walk out? You may ask, "Did you not just say do not take one who will suck the life out of you and leave you high and dry?" Well, I did. The difference is, if God has destined you for this person, most likely the person knows who they are, where they are, where they are going, and how to get there. This person may actually be halfway there and need just a little push as ordained by God.

Parasites

Parasites have no clue about life. They don't know who they are, where they are, or where they are going. Regardless, they believe they are the best thing that has happened to mankind since

Adam and Eve. A male parasite thinks between his legs and never with his head. He may be a dreamer, at best, but has no clue how to achieve those dreams. His plan is to win the mega-lottery and take money from every high-achieving woman. He will not hold down a job or answer to any authority, but will have the best car (and hope you will help him pay for it). He is willing to live in your house so he can eat. While he is living with you, he may also have one or two other women on the side. He thinks he is the smartest guy in town and cleverly avoids getting caught while he cheats. This is no "gem" waiting to be polished… this is a person who should clearly be avoided.

This goes for both men and women. A female parasite owns the world, and her wish is every man's command. Silly men eat out of her hands as she bats her eyelashes and manipulates them. Why should she submit to one man when there are many willing to give her what she wants? She smiles and purrs to get her way and lives only in her universe. The most important thing to her is herself. Men are pawns on her chess board and can be discarded when their usefulness is over. If she does not get her way, she hires other men with her body and discards those who displease her.

I hope you are getting the message. There are "losers" in the world who have no place in our lives. "But what about Christian charity, forgiveness and acceptance?" you may ask. "I can change this person and win them for the Lord!" you might rationalize. Well, unless you are a licensed psychotherapist, you should leave the "parasites" in God's hands. Yes, pray for them, but do not butter their bread. Do not give them access to your kind heart, and don't allow them to sway you with their looks and charm.

Look for substance. There are also many beautiful human beings inside and out who put other people first. The issue is not wealth and beauty, but something that goes way deeper: character.

Think about it.

Sometimes the best things in life are found in hidden places. Sometimes we find a gem in the worst environments. Gold, diamonds, silver, copper, and oil are all buried deep in the belly of the earth. When they are brought up, they go through several processes before they become finished products.

Chapter 11:
Power of Little Things

The difference between passing and failing is one point. One point makes the difference between an "A" and a "B". The difference between "excellent" and "very good" in a well written papers may be crossing the T's. It may be just inserting the correct paragraph in the exact right place.

Small things in life are very powerful. You cannot ignore little things and be successful, whether it's in marriage, raising children, the workplace, personal development, or education. In every area of life, consistently paying attention to details separates high achievers from the average achievers. It's paying attention to the little things that can elevate our lives.

Guard Your Time

Benjamin Franklin wrote, "Do not waste your time; it is the stuff life is made of." If you watch three hours of TV daily from age five, not adding weekends when we watch TV for extended periods of time, that adds up to twenty-one hours a week, eighty-four hours a month, and 1,008, in 12 months and calculates to forty-two days. This does not include the hours we surf the web, text, or talk on the phone.

Guard your time jealously. You can avoid wasting your life by adding value to it. If you earn twenty-five dollars per hour, multiply it by the five years you have wasted watching TV. It may add up to several hundreds of thousands of dollars, if not a million. What can you do with that kind of money? A whole lot!

Weight... and Why We Gain It

If you have struggled with weight all your life, you may need to pay attention to the little things. Gaining weight for most people is all about taking in more calories than you are actually using. I should know, because I have struggled with my weight since childhood. To be able to shed some pounds, we have to ask ourselves why we want to lose weight. If it is just to look good, then we may not succeed. But when we know the health benefits of taking off even five pounds, it becomes easier to lose weight.

Three thousand calories represents one pound of weight. Trying to lose one pound per week becomes easier if we break it down to precisely three hundred calories per day while eating only a quarter of what we used to. If we know that eating one plain glazed donut will cause us to be on the treadmill for two hours to burn off the two to three hundred calories, why eat three donuts? Even ten-calorie candy, soda, or food portions count in weight gain. This is the power of little things. Little steps can make self-sacrifice feel more palatable as we strive to achieve a set goal.

Smart Money

If you make your lunch at home instead of buying $5 Subway sandwiches every day for twenty working days of the week, you will save $100 each month. If you also buy Starbucks coffee at say $3 each morning, you will save $60 a month. Saving $160 a month for one year equals $1,920 and $23,040 for a ten-year period. This can buy you a brand-new car, provide a down payment on a home, and increase in value if you invest it properly. This is money saved by solely making your coffee at home or packing your own lunch.

If you don't have time to use coupons and prefer to not shop at the sale racks, then perhaps you have money to burn. But a frugal person will look for opportunities to save their hard-earned money. It demonstrates good stewardship of the blessings God has given us. Imagine the good you can do in the world simply by spending wisely. In fact, many people are able to tithe simply because they cut unnecessary costs. Luke 6:38 tells us, "Give, and it shall be given unto you; good measure, pressed down, and shaken together, and running over, shall men give unto your bosom. For with the same measure that ye mete withal, it shall be measured to you again."

Spiritual Growth

In your spiritual life, skipping your quiet time for even merely a day takes something out of you. When you skip it three days in a row, you stop missing it. This quiet time is precious and should not be overlooked. It is the perfect time to reflect, pray and be in God's holy presence. If you look at your Bible and its numerous pages, you may not believe someone can finish it in a year. But there are several ways to finish the Bible in as little as ninety days by reading for just fifteen to twenty minutes every day.

Many authors will tell you that the secret to publishing a book is to write consistently, no matter how small, even if it is just few lines. It is more difficult to accomplish this if you are waiting for a big chunk of time to get it done, especially if you are not doing it full time. This reminds me of a preacher who had a method to fully read the New Testament four times in a year, the Psalms and Proverbs every month, and the Old Testament once a year. His plan was simple: read two chapters of the Old Testament, two chapters of the New Testament, a Proverb, and five Psalms every day. I personally followed this plan, and it worked. You will not only finish the Bible, but you will also have the answer for every life question.

These plans are examples of the power of little things. There is no shortcut to spiritual growth. You have to diligently study, pray, listen, and obey to grow spiritually.

In the Workplace

You know that little things are powerful. Do you know that an average worker, between checking e-mails, socializing with coworkers, and applying for other jobs, steals about two to three hours of the eight-hour workday daily? If you calculate that over a forty-hour workweek, it means that an average worker has stolen fifteen hours. When calculated for an employee who earns $50 per hour, that amounts to $750 in a workweek. $1,500, in a two-week pay period, and $39,000 in a year.

You may cringe at this; we all shudder when we see someone holding up a bank, but how often do we rob our employers of time and attention. Both are examples of stealing. One is smarter and the other has a gun, but the outcome is the same.

Most successful relationships are those that make use of precious time. The analogy above shows how we "steal" from employers by goofing off. The same holds true for marriage. Rather than dilly-dallying on useless time wasting endeavors, happily married people spend time together. This may mean sitting on the sofa watching a show, but the point is the husband and wife are side by side enjoying a mutually shared interest.

Little Courtesies

No social media obsession, volunteer work, or any other pursuit should trump the time and effort marriage requires (and deserves). We should not ignore the little courtesies of life—thank you, please, and most of all, I'm sorry. If you have not cultivated these habits, you may not be truly ready for any relationship, let alone a marriage. These little things and the ability to overlook faults make relationships work well. There may not be a perfect relationship, but there are levels of intimacy, understanding, and confidence in marriage. Being aware of what your spouse likes and doing it makes a difference.

Most divorces do not occur because of big issues but are mostly due to the little things. Some relationships do not go to the next level because of little things. Big things just tip over the bucket of accumulated little things. There is a story about Chinese bamboo. This takes five years to sprout, but once it sprouts, it grows ninety feet in just six weeks. For this growth to happen, it must be watered every day. Neglect the watering and you will not see the ninety feet of growth. Likewise, ignoring little things in your marriage will stunt its growth.

The Eye of the Beholder

You see, men are visually sensitive, so trying to look good will be appreciated, though the appreciation may not be verbalized. No one has to break the bank to look good; but, for instance, being mindful of who you are and what colors flatter you can improve your overall look (and outlook). For husbands, there is nothing that melts the heart of a wife more than helpfulness. If a husband wants his wife to respond romantically, "helping" her is often the key. A man who changes lightbulbs, slays bugs, and takes objects out of high shelves is helpful; but a man who makes coffee, scrambles eggs and vacuums the carpet is a prize! Just imagine her response if he cleans the cat litter box and changes diapers!

The Bible says, "Little foxes spoil the vine" (Eccles. 3:2). What little thing are you ignoring in your life that is costing you much? What little things do you need to pay more attention to in order to move from "good" to "excellent" What little courtesy are you ignoring? Who are the people in your life that you owe need a thank-you note? Who has contributed to the growth of your career, spiritual life, wisdom, and outlook? Who do you need to say you are sorry to? Who do you need to forgive?

Leave the Past in the Past

In a marriage, talking about previous relationships might cause your spouse to think he or she is competing with memories. This may not be spoken, but it can come back in unexplained anger, antagonism or even jealousy. Do not let your past life cloud a present relationship. Forget your yesterday and live now.

It is very important to deal with everything in your past, especially traumatic experiences. If you don't deal with it, it will deal with you and severely affect your present and your future. If you need to talk to a pastor or a counselor, do so. Don't ignore it. Addressing such issues allows you to grow from it. Giant leaps are made when your past is resolved and you focus on the "now" and "tomorrow."

Small things in life are very powerful. You cannot ignore little things and be successful, whether it's in marriage, raising children, the workplace, personal development, or education. It's paying attention to the little things that can elevate our lives together.

Chapter 12:
Expectations

As we seriously consider choosing a life partner, another issue we should think through is our expectation of marriage. What are we expecting marriage to be? A bed of roses? A life of peace and harmony, with no ups and downs, no sickness but perfect health, a wellspring of income that will not run dry, being within the upper class in the community, or another Cinderella story? Sometimes life throws us a curveball. What are you going to do then? Will your vows become, "For better to stay, for worse to go"?

It is always good to keep a positive attitude and believe that everything will end well by God's grace. But what if it doesn't? What are you going to do? For instance, it is a known fact that in protracted illness and disease conditions, marriages fail more frequently when the patient is the wife. I guess this happens because the husbands did not expect their wives to become ill, and are not prepared to fill the role of caretaker. But what if the husband was the sick person? Would he expect the woman to leave? Are you going to walk away from your marriage just because things have become unstable or you are in a storm? This important topic should be discussed prior to marriage, don't you think?

When Expectations Fail

Neither the husband nor wife should give up on the other when they are needed most. Still, human nature being what it is, there is always a possibility of such things happening. For example, a nurse once told a story about a patient she had twenty-five years ago. Her patient married when her husband had nothing of offer but himself. They built up a business from scratch and raised four successful kids. Then the wife was stricken with cancer and had a mastectomy. The man left her because he could not live with a woman without a breast. He married another person. My question is, if this man had one or both legs amputated, would he have wanted this woman to support and love him? This man took what he was not willing to give.

Disappointment comes when expectations are not met. What, then, should one reasonably expect? No one prays for bad things to happen, but on this side of eternity we will always face difficult situations. The pathways of life have potholes. We all navigate elevated terrain: valleys and straight routes. Will you forsake your destination just because there are twists and turns and bumps in the road? I don't think so. You will keep driving until you arrive at your intended destination. Please discuss this with whomever you are considering for marriage.

Do Unto Others…

The truth about Christian marriage is precisely what Jesus said in Matthew 6:11, "In this life, you will have tribulation." We will all have challenging situations and circumstances at one time or another. If it is not emotional trouble, it will be trouble with our health, finances, friendships or children. Inevitably, we will face challenges that require us to stand by our partners. It is reasonable to expect our spouses to be there for us when we need them, as well. Look at it this way. If we are tempted to leave our spouses when there is a job loss, then we should not complain when they walk out on us when we lose ours.

Having unrealistic expectations is a good way to become quickly dissatisfied. Each partner must know and respect the expectations they have in place as a couple. Fairness, reciprocity and transparency are "musts" in a relationship. In an extreme example, say you want to cheat, is it acceptable for the other to cheat also (though that word should never be mentioned in a Christian marriage)? If a coworker knows more about you than your spouse, is it an emotional affair? Will the other spouse be permitted to do the same?

A man asked his professional colleague if it was possible for a man to be faithful to his wife. The one answering said that it certainly was possible to stay faithful. But the one asking the question disagreed, despite the fact that he went to church. His reason for being unfaithful to his wife was because… wait for it … his sexual prowess would "help" the single ladies out. What a giant ego wrapped in an excuse! I wonder whether he expected his wife to also help some unmarried men in that way. Let us not expect of others what we cannot give to them.

Be Realistic

Why is expectation important in a book about marriage? Let me illustrate this with another story. A husband had a very good friend with whom he discussed every serious business decision, rather than discussing them with his wife. The friend rubbed her nose in it, took every opportunity to start a conversation with something like, "Has your husband told you yet about this project or that?" The woman tried to explain to her husband that his relationship with his friend hurt their marriage and threatened their business. If the roles were reversed, how would the husband have felt?

At first her husband did not see the problem, until he learned the hard way. His friend betrayed him. Yes, the trusted "friend" started his own business — by coaxing away the husband's employees. As you can imagine, the husband apologized to his wife and learned, too late, the wisdom of her advice.

Emotional Affair

If while you are single you have a very close friendship with someone of the opposite sex, nothing intimate, but just someone whom you confide in and vice versa, is it reasonable to dial back on that relationship when you become engaged to marry another? Nothing is wrong with this relationship if the one who has this friend will not feel bad if the partner also has a close friend of the opposite sex. You may find out that a man may not be comfortable with his future bride having a friendship with another man but may want to keep his female friend. This is not a reasonable expectation. Some people may keep you as the stand-by person just in case the plan for the one they are really after doesn't work out. When they know that some else is interested in you, they become more visible and create a subtle competitive atmosphere. If you are not smart, you fall for this feigned interest till the one who is really serious walks out. It is unrealistic to expect that this "friend" has anything good for you. This happens more often in very long- standing relationships.

If you are married and you have a friend who knows your hopes and aspirations more than your spouse, you call them first when you have good or bad news, you may be having an emotional affair. You may not even realize it; the test of this though, is your feeling when you find out that you are not the first in your spouse's life but the second.

While dating, it does not hurt to discuss our expectations before things get serious. That way, when the issue of marriage comes up, we will be able to make a decision without regret. There are many other topics, such as whether it's reasonable to have a joint bank account when you are married. You have to find out what will work out for your future family. Not having this understanding will likely be a bone of contention in the future.

Fair and Balanced

For those who are expected to help with siblings or with aging parents, it is fair to do for one set of in-laws as you do for the other set. If you expect your spouse to send money to your family, he/she should expect it of you too. One lady inherited a stepdaughter who was in college. At the time, the woman was working, but her spouse was not. Both were supporting the stepdaughter in college. The woman, who worked a twelve-hour shift, would get up very early in the morning to get her three preschool children ready, take them to day care, pick them up on her way back, cook, feed, and bathe them, and send them to bed. This happened during school semesters and even on holidays.

You are probably wondering about the whereabouts of her husband and her step-daughter, since she juggled so many responsibilities and used her money to pay for daycare and college. If the roles were reversed, would the man or step-daughter have done the same for this woman? How long did they expect her to continue living like that? Clearly they were taking advantage of the definition of a "good wife." If this woman dropped dead unexpectedly, people would say she was a very good wife and very supportive of her husband who inadvertently sent her to an early grave. If the scenario applied to the husband's daughter or sister, would he have wanted her to die slowly because she was married to a man who was not ready to give, but lived just to take? This also happens when roles are reversed. What is a reasonable expectation in marriage?

Family Dynamics

A man who was his mother's only child married a woman who did not want her widowed mother-in-law to visit. She felt her home was "her" territory. Now, it is true that she can decide who can and who cannot visit. But what did she expect her husband to do—love her more for creating a gap between him and his mother?

If the roles were reversed and the woman was the sole daughter of a widower, how would she feel if her spouse announced that her father was no longer welcome to their home? Better still, what if you were a parent and had an in-law that did not want your company? How would you feel? It is time to open our eyes to the dynamics between parents and children. It is true that a man should leave his father and mother to cleave to his wife, so that they may be joined as one. However, it is also true that we are commanded to honor our mothers and fathers. Leaving and cleaving should be understood and exercised in the context of purpose: one can chase a thousand but two 10, 000, (Deut 32:30). Let's explore this further.

Raising Children

Some men, but mostly women, raise their children single handedly. This ingrained sense of responsibility is based on the Bible verse that says it is difficult for a woman to forget the child she bore. Therefore, single parents especially mothers work three jobs and deny themselves nearly everything to make sure their children are provided for. They sometimes endure toxic work environment for years, just to have financial stability and keep roofs over their children's head.

Why then would anyone expect that after all that suffering, that these parents who sacrificed so much do not deserve to be around their children? If the person coming into this family would momentarily put themselves in the shoes of this parent and walk a mile in it, maybe, they would have an idea of what it takes to raise a child. Please do not allow anyone to force you to forget your parents no matter what. Do not help anyone forget their parents. If anything, you should strive to be the peace maker where there is a misunderstanding. Obviously there are several dynamics to every marriage, situation, and circumstance.

No two circumstances can be one hundred percent the same, but the underlying facts remain the same. You receive what you dish out. You get what you give. Some ladies say they will not marry any man if his mother is still alive. Some mothers-in-law vow to destroy their sons' marriages. Some people are not reasonable, and this is an indication that their hearts are not Christ-centered.

Aim for "Parallel"

Be smart and let each spouse handle their parent. Do for your parent-in-law what you would do for your own parents. Live with a clear conscience before God and let him be your defense. Trying to defend yourself just makes it worse. Plotting revenge makes it worse. Instead, strive for balance.

The bottom line is that the relationship should be parallel. There is room in a husband's life for both his wife and mother. The two most important women in his life should not impose on each other. This ensures their beloved husband/son will live happily and healthily, with family member knowing their place in the household structure. Out of love for a husband/son, mothers and daughter-in-law should know intuitively when they have crossed the line. A husband/son should not have to play referee when Christ guides family relationships.

Talking Points

This is an important talking point prior to marriage. What are you expecting to give and what are you expecting to receive in return? Be sure and discuss these types of family dynamics before tying the knot! And remember, just as we want others to be objective, we should be objective. Just as we want others to be fair, we should be fair. We are made new in Christ... and we should act like it. The issue of expectation can be summed up in the words of Christ, which say, "Therefore, all things whatsoever ye would that men should do to you, do ye, even so, to them: for this is the law and the prophets" (Matt. 7:12 NIV).

More advice: be very careful when you enter a new family. You are the stranger in the family. You may be tested. New relatives may try to lure you into gossip. They may try to stir the pot. Your spouse's siblings may try to reveal secrets, scandals, old wounds and feuds. Avoid it. Deal with each person as an individual. Remember that a sibling can say whatever they want about a sibling... but will turn on you if you chime in. It will never matter that the other person started the conversation. You will take the fall. The best solution is to never talk about someone unless you can say the same to their face.

Clarify and discuss these scenarios before marriage. Lay out expectations and be prepared to give what you are expecting.

Children

Do you want to have children? How many? These are issues to discuss well before tying the knot. If you had hysterectomy and want to a man who plans on having six children, you should make sure he understands that adoption or surrogacy are the other options. There are women who are infertile due to a medical condition, or barren due to a medical procedure, who, conveniently forget to mention it. What do they expect their husbands to do after the fact? If, on the other hand, a man had an irreversible vasectomy and is getting married to a woman who really wants kids, he should reveal his condition. There are men who fail to mention that very important detail. What do they expect their wives to do when they find out? Honesty, certainly, is the best policy.

There are a thousand families with the above-raised issues who are happily married parents of wonderful adopted children — because they loved each other for who they are. Deception is a faulty foundation for marriage, much like building a house on marshy ground. Flee from deceit, as it is the path to heartache disunity.

Here's a story about a family who knows the heartbreak of deception first hand. They were very good Christians and had been married for sixteen years. The husband had a very low sperm count and was infertile. He met a college student who preyed on him to help finance her education. He fell for the seduction not knowing she had a boyfriend who had gotten her pregnant. She announced to the married man that he was the father of the baby. He bought the story and eventually moved the pregnant girl in, while his wife of sixteen years moved out. The girl carried the pregnancy and had the baby. However, when the baby's genotype was checked, the man discovered it was not his baby.

A similar incident happened over twenty years ago overseas. A man had five children and wanted to send his children outside the country for the summer holidays. During the health screening for the visas, it was discovered that only the first child was the man's child. The rest of the children were fathered by another person. He never had marital problems with his wife; so imagine his surprise and devastation. There are things that cannot be hidden from a spouse, especially if you want to stay married for life.

Think about it.

Disappointment comes when expectations are not met.

Chapter 13:
Prejudices

Webster defines prejudice as, "Injury or damage resulting from some judgment or action of another in disregard of one's rights, especially detriment to one's legal rights or claims."[2] Dictionary.com defines it as, "Unfavorable opinion or feeling formed beforehand or without knowledge, thought or reason."[3] In social psychology, prejudice is an unjustified or incorrect attitude (usually negative) toward an individual based solely on an individual's membership of a social group.

What place does prejudice have in a Christian marriage book? A lot! We all have prejudices and preconceived notions. The challenge is to understand why, and balance our views against Biblical principles. After all, we probably mingle on a daily basis with others who have different religions, ethnicities, cultures, races, or social circles.

Many of our learned behaviors and attitudes generally come from our home orientation. Parents, peers and politics may affect our views. It can all affect the marriage union. Again, honestly discussing our prejudices with our future spouse can help put out a fire before it starts. It's always best to be on the same page, or at least understand the other's viewpoint.

---

[2] http://www.merriam-webster.com/dictionary/prejudice.

[3] http://dictionary.reference.com/browse/prejudice.

Unequally Yoked

The Bible clearly says, "Do not be unequally yoked together with unbelievers. For what fellowship has righteousness with lawlessness? And what communion has light with darkness?" (2 Cor. 6:14).

Is this prejudice? No, it is Biblical advice. We are to share the Gospel with unbelievers, but we don't need to marry them to do so. In fact, being unequally yoked has consequences, as the Bible clearly warns. But many disregard the Bible, and think they can "change" an unbeliever after marriage. They convince themselves that their spouses will convert. Not so fast! Do not make this assumption! Who you marry is who you get, and if anything, a person's true nature comes out after wedlock.

This may be an extreme example, but if you marry someone who participates in ancestral worship or voodoo rituals, this obviously goes against everything you believe. Think of having to live with a rat in your house because your spouse believes that a family member was reincarnated as a rat. Think about sleeping with a Python in the same room because your spouse's ancestors worshiped it. Not every "cultural norm" is compatible with a Christian lifestyle. Be sure to discuss belief systems and views prior to marriage. It's important to know the influences your potential mate has been raised with and exposed to. Talk it out and weigh it against the word of God. And no matter how much you love this person... love God's word more.

Ethnicities

Regarding ethnic prejudices, it is becoming more acceptable to inter-marry within nationalities and racial groups. In Christ, we all have a common ground that is color blind. But if you are in a serious biracial relationship, you will (most likely) face a certain amount of prejudice and stereotyping. You'll encounter relatives and friends who have their own prejudices. The children you bring into the world may be on the receiving end of cruelty from others.

What if your parents prefer that you marry an unbeliever from your race rather than a believer from another race? What will you do? God's word says that we are to stand firm in our Christian beliefs and values. The culture that truly matters comes from Jesus' teachings. That is what binds a couple together, and they may have to reject certain cultural practices that run counter to Biblical principles. Remember, culture is manmade. Christianity is Jesus-made.

Under the Microscope

As mentioned before, culture can be a huge factor in a successful marriage. Each culture has its own views about marriage, and it's wise to examine the implications. Couples owe it to themselves to study their differences closely. This ensures compatibility, provides a level of expectation and a plain field for cooperation and harmony.

For instance, you may be from a paternal society where the man pays a bride price or dowry. Your significant other may be from a maternal society where the woman brings the bride price or dowry. What are you going to do? What if a bride doesn't want to change her last name? How will that influence your union? What if you belong to different denominations? Do you expect your future spouse to leave his or her place of worship? What if he or she cannot compromise on that? What if you are about to marry someone in a higher economic status, and it is causing friction between you and the rest of the family members? Will you and your future spouse love and support each other enough to survive the whispers, innuendos, and suspicion from the rest of the family?

What "prejudice" are you unwilling to give up? What if your spouse is not willing to compromise under any circumstance?

One daytime talk show introduced the neighborhood swingers who swapped wives in exclusive clubs. If you are getting married to someone who sees nothing wrong with that, don't be surprised if he or she asks you to be a part of it. What if your spouse wants you to have an intimate relationship with a business associate to be awarded a multimillion-dollar contract? What if your spouse would, literally, sell his or her own own soul for a profit? He/she may take out life insurance and kill you for it. Such people are not worth going into a relationship with. Find out beforehand if your prospective partner favors such arrangements. Isn't it better to know (and avoid) such upfront?

Quality Matters

"Who can know the heart of man?" asks the Bible (Jer. 17:9, KJV). Do you know your own heart? Before you tie the knot, you must look deep inside and examine your preconceived notions. It allows you to operate from a position of strength, knowledge, and expectation.

Have you ever asked yourself what kind of spouse you want? If you were asked the qualities you wanted in a bride or groom, could you name ten off the top of your head? It is wise to actually consider what we want in our mate. It's especially helpful to know ourselves, because then are we able to choose a spouse that complements who we are.

The saying goes, "One man's food is another man's poison" or "One man's trash is another man's treasure." The point is, each person's "personality" makeup is distinctive and relative. Situations and circumstances are different. Everyone should make sure that whatever prejudices and perceptions they have—be they of other cultures, ethnicities, religions, and mannerisms—should be their own and with good Biblical reasons, and not because of another person's prejudices or opinions.

Take a piece of paper and write down twenty qualities you want in a spouse, then list your own qualities according to the level of importance to you. This will help unveil your prejudices, preconceived notions and ingrained attitudes. Compare them to God's word. Then be honest about what you will or will not tolerate in a marriage relationship.

Think about it.

Many of our learned behaviors and attitudes mostly come from our homes of orientation. Your prejudices and resentments should be your own and with good reasons, not because of another person's prejudices or opinions.

Chapter 14:
Shopping and Choosing

How nice if there was a place on this planet where men and women were kept on the shelf and people were allowed to choose what they wanted, like selecting apples from the grocery store. If you were browsing in the Wife/Husband Shop, would you know who to pick?

Of course there is no such spousal shopping mall, but there are several types of men and women who are ready to settle down. So the first question we should ask ourselves is, "Am I a "wife" or a "husband" material?" The second question we should ask ourselves, when making a selection, is, "Is he or she a wife or a husband material?

You have to be properly prepared to be husband material and take home a good wife... and vice versa. You have to decide who the right person is for you. This is important, because who you marry is what you get. Tying the knot won't necessarily change someone for the better. If anything, the real person will come out after you have married.

We will look at prospective wives and husbands

Different Types of Women

Men, have choices. What types of women sit on the shelf, and which are the best picks?

The Clinging Vine: This type of wife has no mind of her own and will not sweep her house until she is told to do so. She is so needy that she tolerates abuse and thinks she is not good enough for any other lifestyle. She needs constant encouragement and withdraws into a shell when she does not receive positive affirmation. She cannot hold a conversation independently and is fearful of offending, and therefore does not voice her opinion. She may not even realize she is being trampled upon. Truth is, many responsible and intelligent men need partners they can have a conversation with.

Nagging/Contentious Wife: Delilah (Judges 16)

Proverbs 25:24 states, "Better to live on a corner of the roof than share a house with a quarrelsome wife" (NIV). This kind of woman is contentious and complains about every single thing. If you get her a present, she complains; if you do not, she complains. If you call to check on her mom, she asks why; if you don't, she asks why not. If you stay home, she needs her breathing space; if you go out, she complains you are never at home. The book of Proverbs likens this kind of woman to a dripping faucet or a leaking roof on a rainy day. We see in the book of Judges chapter 16 an excellent example:

> 4 And it came to pass afterward, that he loved a woman in the valley of Sorek, whose name was Delilah.
>
> 5 And the lords of the Philistines came up unto her, and said unto her, Entice him, and see wherein his great strength lieth, and by what means we may prevail against him, that we may bind him to afflict him; and we will give thee every one of us eleven hundred pieces of silver.
>
> 6 And Delilah said to Samson, Tell me, I pray thee, wherein thy great strength lieth, and wherewith thou mightest be bound to afflict thee.
>
> 7 And Samson said unto her, If they bind me with seven green withs that were never dried, then shall I be weak, and be as another man.
>
> 8 Then the lords of the Philistines brought up to her seven green withs which had not been dried, and she bound him with them.

9 Now there were men lying in wait, abiding with her in the chamber. And she said unto him, The Philistines be upon thee, Samson. And he brake the withs, as a thread of tow is broken when it toucheth the fire. So his strength was not known.

10 And Delilah said unto Samson, Behold, thou hast mocked me, and told me lies: now tell me, I pray thee, wherewith thou mightest be bound.

11 And he said unto her, If they bind me fast with new ropes that never were occupied, then shall I be weak, and be as another man.

12 Delilah therefore took new ropes, and bound him therewith, and said unto him, The Philistines be upon thee, Samson. And there were liers in wait abiding in the chamber. And he brake them from off his arms like a thread.

13 And Delilah said unto Samson, Hitherto thou hast mocked me, and told me lies: tell me wherewith thou mightest be bound. And he said unto her, If thou weavest the seven locks of my head with the web.

14 And she fastened it with the pin, and said unto him, The Philistines be upon thee, Samson. And he awaked out of his sleep, and went away with the pin of the beam, and with the web.

15 And she said unto him, How canst thou say, I love thee, when thine heart is not with me? thou hast mocked me these three times, and hast not told me wherein thy great strength lieth.

16 And it came to pass, when she pressed him daily with her words, and urged him, so that his soul was vexed unto death;

17 That he told her all his heart, and said unto her, There hath not come a razor upon mine head; for I have been a Nazarite unto God from my mother's womb: if I be shaven, then my strength will go from me, and I shall become weak, and be like any other man.

18 And when Delilah saw that he had told her all his heart, she sent and called for the lords of the Philistines, saying, Come up this once, for he hath shewed me all his heart. Then the lords of the Philistines came up unto her, and brought money in their hand.

19 And she made him sleep upon her knees; and she called for a man, and she caused him to shave off the seven locks of his head; and she began to afflict him, and his strength went from him.

20 And she said, The Philistines be upon thee, Samson. And he awoke out of his sleep, and said, I will go out as at other times before, and shake myself. And he wist not that the LORD was departed from him.

21 But the Philistines took him, and put out his eyes, and brought him down to Gaza, and bound him with fetters of brass; and he did grind in the prison house, (KJV)

Vitriolic: Herodias

She is described as the "Tabasco sauce" or "Habanero" wife. She is okay until she gets furious. You cannot predict what will set her off. Everyone walks on eggshells because she may throw a knife, call you the scum of the earth, tear up her wedding photos, and pour hot soup on the nearest person. When that moment of madness passes, she will be sorry and make it up to you… if you are still alive. She leaves emotional scars and your children, parents and friends will not be spared. Everyone around you knows their life is in danger if her toes are stepped on. A perfect example of this kind of spouse will be Herodias. She requested the head of John the Baptist because, he told Herod it was not right for him to marry his brother's wife.

At that time Herod the tetrarch heard of the fame of Jesus,

2 And said unto his servants, This is John the Baptist; he is risen from the dead; and therefore mighty works do shew forth themselves in him.

3 For Herod had laid hold on John, and bound him, and put

him in prison for Herodias' sake, his brother Philip's wife.

4 For John said unto him, It is not lawful for thee to have her.

5 And when he would have put him to death, he feared the multitude, because they counted him as a prophet.

6 But when Herod's birthday was kept, the daughter of Herodias danced before them, and pleased Herod.

7 Whereupon he promised with an oath to give her whatsoever she would ask.

8 And she, being before instructed of her mother, said, Give me here John the Baptist's head in a charger.

9 And the king was sorry: nevertheless for the oath's sake, and them which sat with him at meat, he commanded it to be given her.

10 And he sent, and beheaded John in the prison.

11 And his head was brought in a charger, and given to the damsel: and she brought it to her mother, (Mathew 14 1-11, KJV)

The Queen Mother: Jezebel

I call these types of woman "Jezebel's daughters" and "Jezebel's sisters".It is their way or the highway. They decide who you talk to, when you talk to them, what you wear, which person you are going to be friendly with, and when you talk to your family members. Women like this wear the pants, whether you bring home a fatter check or not. They are the head, and you are the tail. They are like this with every relationship, not just with you. Those who disagree or fail to comply become a target of malicious retribution. Beware, because this type of woman divides to rule and is loud, obnoxious and totally self-absorbed. She will be nice only when she needs something from you. In your group of friends, she sets herself and family on top and look down on the rest. She will try to suggest that she is doing you a favor by taking something from you. The story of what Jezebel did can be found in 1Kings 21: 1-15. She killed an innocent man for his inheritance.

The Real Deal: Micah Saul's Daughter

Some women beautifully mirror the example of the "Proverbs 31" woman. Simply put, they are down-to-earth, intelligent, and compassionate. They know what they want, love all, and are well respected. You learn from this type of woman, but she does not rub it in. She is also willing to ask when she doesn't know something. She protects her spouse and family. Micah was Saul the King's daughter who loved David. Saul, wanted to kill David because of Jealousy; and at the risk of her own life she advised her husband to run away. David would have been killed if not for how God used her to let him down through the window. She also made scathing remarks David when he danced heartily before the Ark of the Lord. Micah qualifies as a good wife because she defied the King's command at the risk of her own life to save her husband. This story is found in 1 Samuel 19.

These symbolize several kinds of wives you can pick up off the shelf of life. Which one are you going to take home with you?

Different Types of Men

Once you know the inventory, you can make the most intelligent pick. Below are general descriptions of various types of men.

Authoritarian: Nabal

He is heartless, treats his wife as a house maid. He has no fear of God, government, man, or woman. Trying to reason with him after he's made a decision is useless. He is stubborn and arrogant and will not listen to anyone. He may be a good provider for his family, but his wife will have no say in any decision in the house. He will choose her friends and decide when and where she can go. Any attempts by her to do otherwise, it would result in fights, both physical and verbal. To avoid this, the woman may simply give in. A typical example is Nabal as described in 1 Samuel Chapter 25. Please look up this reference so that you will have an insight into the characters of Men like this. Avoid them like a plague.

Spineless Husband: Ahab

At the opposite end of the spectrum is the husband who really has no mind of his own. He is like a reed that bends with the wind's direction. Anyone can tell him what to do. He has no philosophies about life. He cannot make up his own mind; and he favors whoever is present. It's easy to convince him to do anything, even if it comes at the expense of his spouse. He may work hard, but will give his money to whoever cries the loudest to him at the expense of his family's needs. He'll complain if another person does not do the same for him. This guy just wants to be "Mr. Nice" and does not know how to say no.

Bible unfolds the story of Ahab who is a typical example of one who has no mind of his own in 1Kings 21.

God's Gift to Women: Solomon

Some men are "Prima Donnas" who think they are the best thing to happen on planet earth. They may be very pleasant to the eyes, but that is all there is. They won't work, since their "job" is to look good and feed off women. To this kind of man, women are merely toys, and once used, interest is lost. In fact, this is the "parasite" mentioned in a previous chapter. He hops from one woman to another to maintain a lifestyle. As a husband, he is extremely selfish and could care less about fulfilling the needs of his spouse physically, emotionally, or spiritually. These men are the center of attention and in love with themselves only. While Solomon was very wise, he had a passion for women. It was said that Solomon had 700 wives and 300 concubines, (1 Kings 11:3). Imagine being one of his wives. How could he truly love any of them?

Teenager in the Body of 32 Year Old:

This type of man stopped growing emotionally and is still a teenager, though chronologically he is in his thirties. As a husband, he'll never say sorry; will stop talking to the spouse when there is a quarrel, or will refuse to eat food. He is used to his mother taking care of him and will not help out around the house. He expects you to work two jobs, pick up after him, keep the house clean, and feed the children fed, but will not lift a finger to help. His sees his children as competition for his wife's affection. He's a nag and a critic. He'll send money to his own parents, but not yours. He may throw fits and beat his children… and you.

Real Deal

Some men do all they can to make ends meet. They are willing to discuss issues with their spouses. They know they are not faultless and own up to their mistakes. They do not expect perfection from their wives or hold shortcomings over their heads. They respect their parents-in-law as they respect their own. This type of man tries to help out when he can and makes sure everyone in the family is taken care of. He is a cheerleader, appreciates your gifts and talents, and never sees you as a competition… but as a completion. He is reasonable when he disagrees with your assessment of the situation.

Now you know the inventory, who would you like to take off the shelf and settle down with?

Choices

As you read through available types of husbands and wives, did you identify which one you are first? As the Bible states, wives are found and husbands do the searching. As a woman, who do you want to find you? Who are you searching for? If you are also weighed on a balance, will you perfectly complement your choice? This time of waiting is an opportunity to think through what and who you want as a spouse, and also what kind of spouse you want to be.

In real life, each person may have a little mix of every trait, but will obviously have a strong inclination toward one of the attributes mentioned above. Identify the qualities that are more tolerable to you and avoid a closer relationship with someone who has traits you dislike.

Don't let loneliness cause you to make a bad choice. Keep busy with the Lord's work, especially reading the Scriptures. After all, once you are married you may not be able to read as much due to family obligations. Volunteering for good causes is another way of spending time with other people. Traveling, if you are able to, will help you see the world and learn about other cultures. Learn a vocation in other areas than your field and widen your horizon even more. Find a hobby, or better yet, a paid hobby (writing, sewing, artwork, baking e.t.c). Why not advance your education or take certification courses in your trade?

While you are single, be objective with yourself and determine if there is an area in your life that needs to change for the better. When we deal with our weaknesses, we position ourselves for higher achievements. Being single provides a period of personal development and self-refinement that prepares us for marriage. Being single allows us to make better choices when contemplating potential spouses.

Think about it.

Being single provides a period of personal development and self-refinement that prepares us for marriage.

Chapter 15:
Philosophy of Life

The Oxford Dictionary has two definitions for philosophy, but for the purpose of this discussion, we will focus on the one that says, "A theory and attitude that acts as a guiding principle for behavior." Do you have a philosophy that guides your life? How did you acquire it—from your parents, your coach, or other people whose opinions you respect? Without a personal philosophy, you may be among the millions of people who wake up every day eat, work, and sleep with no clue about why they are here on this planet.

What is Your Life's Mission?

Can you answer the question, "What is your life's mission?" Without a doubt, it has something to do with God's divine plan, as described in Jeremiah 1:5:

Before I formed you in the womb I knew you; before you were born I sanctified you; I ordained you a prophet to the nations. For you formed my inward parts; you covered me in my mother's womb. I will praise you, for I am fearfully and wonderfully made Marvelous are your works, And that my soul knows very well. My frame was not hidden from you, When I was made in secret, And skillfully wrought in the lowest parts of the earth Your eyes saw my substance, being yet unformed. And in Your book they all were written, The days fashioned for me, When as yet there were none of them. (Ps. 139:13–16)

These passages imply that God knows each and every one of the more than seven billion people on earth. He knows the gifts and talents he placed inside each of us, and he expects a return on his investment. Your frustration come from not being in the place he appointed you to be. You cannot accomplish your mission if you do not know what it is. Pray and ask God to direct you. Ask him to use you for the greater good. Once you know what your mission is, set short-term and long-term goals to accomplish it.

Prepare for the Mission

What we did yesterday brought us to where we are today, and what we do now will take us to some other place tomorrow. It's all a part of preparing for the mission.

This brings us to our daily habits. How are you using your time and your money? Are you spending everything to keep up with the Joneses? Are you using some of it to invest in yourself through reading, traveling, offering and attending seminars, or whatever? What are you doing to make yourself more valuable? Are you increasing your intellectual worth? Are you focused on your spiritual growth? What guides your behavior? How has it helped you in the past? Can you do better with a little change? How honest are you with yourself? What lies have you told yourself?

I ask myself these questions every day and have made changes that have helped me reach some goals. Changing for the better is good; because one day we will come face-to-face with our Maker. When we do, will he say, "Well done, good and faithful servant," or will he say, "You were supposed to slay giants, but you let unnecessary fears back you into a corner"?

Mercy and Forgiveness

Last but not least, Romans 3:23 states that we have all have sinned and fallen short of the glory of God. I am very grateful to our God of a million chances. He gives us opportunity to climb out of the holes we dig ourselves into. God takes our messes and turns them into messages; the tests of our lives become testimonies. His grace is sufficient; therefore, our failures teach us lessons and become lessons for others.

Likewise, our philosophy of marriage should include mercy and forgiveness. We are to emulate Christ's example. We are tasked to do our utmost for our spouses, and ask forgiveness when we fall short. Our spouses are to do the same. This humble spirit will go far in drawing us closer to each other and to the Lord.

Think about it.

What we did yesterday brought us to where we are today, and what we do now will take us to some other place tomorrow.

Chapter 16:
Definition of a Successful Marriage

No two individuals are exactly alike, and even identical twins have differences. No couple replicates the exact same personal philosophies or individual definitions about life. This is why each marriage is unique. Couples must develop their own definition of a successful marriage by asking the hard questions, soul searching, and agreeing on expectations.

The "Ideal"

We all want a spouse who can be counted upon, someone who can be described with many adjectives; trustworthy, faithful, forgiving, honest, respectful, grateful, supportive and nurturing. The question is, do we demonstrate those same qualities ourselves? Do we walk the talk?

The most successful marriages include husbands and wives who hold themselves accountable. No one is perfect, not by any means. But that doesn't mean we can't try to be perfect! Well-adjusted couples strive daily to demonstrate personal standards of morality, ethics, and honor... and apologize when they fall short. The bottom line is that they would gladly give their lives to spare each other and their children from harm. This deep, deep devotion mirrors Christ's sacrifice for us — a Biblical marriage at its finest.

Opposites Attract

That being said, we have to deal with the realities. Some days the dazzling adjectives are missing in action. At those times, our marriages may fall short of the "ideal." The truth is, we are human and flawed. We each have strengths and weaknesses. The upside is that, many times, a husband's strength is his wife's weakness, and a wife's strength is her husband's weakness. Therefore, they fill in the missing components and complete each other. In this case, opposites do attract.

For instance, if your spouse is great on demonstrating affection but cannot keep the house clean, is this a deal breaker? What if you are a stickler for bookkeeping, and your husband can't manage to save a receipt? In reality, what may be very important to one person may be unimportant to another. The good thing is that you can work together to achieve whatever you want.

The fact is, some days your marriage may be blissful, and other days it may be a struggle. However, when you have your own working definition of success, both you and your spouse can pool strengths to minimize weaknesses.

Wealth Is Not Everything

A successful marriage stands on a statement frequently included in marriage vows: "For richer and poorer." Finances are fluid. A hefty bank account may be temporary. The only certainty in life is uncertainty; and material wealth should never be the sole premise for accepting a wedding proposal.

A prominent lady once said on Sixty Minutes that it was better to be unhappy in the back of a limousine than joyful on a back of a bicycle. Another person may say, "I would rather be poor and happily married than be sorrowful in a wealthy, but toxic, relationship." Am I implying that wealth and marriage don't mix? By no means! I'm just saying that one should not be solely dependent on the other.

For instance, if your spouse is a professional athlete, you can't really complain when he or she travels. You should know from the beginning that in order to earn a spectacular salary, your spouse will be gone for days, weeks, or months. You should also know that a career in sports is short-lived, and that life in the arena will eventually end. If you don't save and invest, your riches will turn to rags. Will your marriage be any less when a financial crisis hits?

Or will your marriage continue to thrive despite a downturn in your bank account?

What have you built your marriage upon — dollars or love?

Drive the Posted Speed Limit!

A very wise minister once said that marriage could be compared to driving on the freeway. If you drive the speed of the person in front of you, you may be speeding or going slower than the speed limit. If you go according to the posted speed limit, you will be sure that there won't be any flashing lights following you. So "go the posted speed limit". In this case, trust what is written in the Bible. Ecclesiastes 4:9–12 paints a picture of what a Christian marriage union looks like:

Two are better than one, because they have a good return for their labor: If either of them falls down, one can help the other up. But pity anyone who falls and has no one to help them up. Also, if two lie down together, they will keep warm. But how can one keep warm alone? Though one may be overpowered, two can defend themselves. A cord of three strands is not quickly broken. (NIV)

Think about it.

No two individuals are exactly alike, and even identical twins have differences. No couple replicates the exact same personal philosophies or individual definitions about life. This is why each marriage is unique.

Chapter 17:
The Last Chapter

There is a saying, that "We make plans and God laughs." In other words, we may think we are in control… but in reality, God is in control. He knows every future pathway we'll travel. He has a personalized plan for each and every one of his children.

Be Rooted

Perhaps your group of friends have all wedded and settled down… except you. That does not mean in any way that you did something wrong and God is punishing you. It also does not mean time is running out. It simply means you are part of God's future plan. In fact, you may be one to raise godly offspring one day who will bring him glory. But how can you root your offspring in the Word when you, the teacher, are not rooted? Ye of little faith! Perhaps this time of waiting is happening to give you time to root.

Yes, God is giving you an opportunity to draw closer to him. Whether you are married or not, the door to his kingdom is open to you. There is no sin that he cannot forgive. Perhaps you have been involved in premarital or extramarital sex. God is giving you a chance to come to your senses and stop. In fact, Psalm 33:10–11 says, "The LORD foils the plans of the nations; He thwarts the purposes of the peoples. But the plans of the LORD stand firm forever, the purposes of His heart through all generations" (NIV).

His Plan, Not Yours

In the scripture above, God very plainly refers to His plan — not your plan, not your parent's, plan or that of a principality, or a power — but God's own plans and purposes. Be in his will.

Repent of your sins. Accept Jesus' gift of salvation and follow the narrow path. Allow God to direct every footstep. If the Word of God is true—and it is—there is no earthly drama that can separate us from God's divine plan and purpose.

Our Bible heroes all experienced hardships and passed through the crucible. God brought them out of it. He will bring you out of it, as well. Think of Daniel and his trials. He was one of the royal princes carried away as a captive from Judah by Nebuchadnezzar, king of Babylon. He was made a eunuch and would never have children of his own. He was about to be killed, along with other astrologers from Babylon, over a mad king's dream. Daniel knew the God of heaven and prayed to him. God delivered him in a glorious way. In another episode, Daniel was thrown into a lion's den. But rather than be torn to pieces, God shut the mouths of the lions.

When Daniel's companions, Shadrach, Meshach, and Abednego, refused to bow down to an idol, King Neb had them thrown into a furnace heated up several degrees higher than normal. It was so hot that those who threw the three men into the furnace died. But Shadrach, Meshach, and Abednego emerged alive and well, without even a trace of smoke on their skin. Nebuchadnezzar eventually acknowledged that the God of Daniel was the real God.

Walk by Faith

Undoubtedly, you have faced your own trials. Perhaps the person you courted left you high and dry. Perhaps you were left at the altar. Perhaps you were cheated on. We may think that someone has written the last chapter, but only God is the author of our lives. Whatever disappointments, abandonment or betrayals that have come our way, we can be assured that God's plan has a higher purpose. We may not see it now, but in hindsight we will say, "I did not know that God was preventing me from getting into something bad!" He may have stopped you from walking into hell on earth.

Ecclesiastes 3 talks about times and seasons for everything

under heaven. From my understanding, it means God's own appointed time. Marriage will happen for you precisely it did for your friends and relations. He has made everything beautiful in its time (Eccles. 3:11 NIV). It may be hard, but keep looking to God for goodness and mercy. He is the master planner. He will make all things work together for your good (Romans 8:27 NIV). He is the same yesterday, today, and forever. If he could stop the power of fire and the mouths of lions, I am sure he can put a mate in your path. Can you trust him and walk by faith?

Only God knows your beginning, end, and everything in between. Seek first the kingdom of God and its righteousness, and all these other things shall be added unto you (Matt. 6:33). Abandon yourself to God.

Exercise Your Faith

If you want to exercise faith, go window shopping for a wedding gown or Tuxedo even when there is no one in the picture. That is a step of faith. Take a notepad and plan your wedding. This is a step of faith. And while you wait patiently and plan diligently, let God select his very best for you. He never sleeps nor slumbers. He will not wake up and say, "Oops, I forgot my daughter or my son"

If God is our heavenly Father — and he is — then we can be rest assured that He knows our hearts, our needs, our wants, our longings, our hurts and our hopes.

Think about it.

Only God knows your beginning, end, and everything in between. Remember he is the author of all of them.

Chapter 18:
Oh! Just One More Thing

Next to salvation, the most important decision in your life, is your partner. Choosing correctly will take you to the highest height of your life, and a wrong choice will send you in the opposite direction. Are you ready?

Read ahead for a few additional questions that will help you prepare for marriage.

For Men

Is your emotional maturity able to handle the ups and downs of a marriage relationship? Do you run back to your mother each time you have an argument with someone? Can you afford a home of your own? Are you materially able to take care of a family? Can you deny yourself of some luxuries to put your family's needs first? Have you saved anything for a rainy day? Will you pledge to love your wife the way Christ loves the church?

For Women

Can you keep a home? Thank God for fast food places, but can you cook? Do you know how to clean? What are your goals for raising your children? How are you planning to discipline your children? Are you ready to submit to your husband? Are you willing to let him lead the family? Can you give him control over the final decisions?

Ephesians 5:21–27 says the following:

Submit to one another out of reverence for Christ. Wives,

submit yourselves to your own husbands as you do to the Lord. For the husband is the head of the wife as Christ is the head of the church, his body, of which he is the Savior. Now as the church submits to Christ, so also wives should submit to their husbands in everything. Husbands, love your wives, just as Christ loved the church and gave himself up for her to make her holy, cleansing her by the washing with water through the word, and to present her to himself as a radiant church, without stain or wrinkle or any other blemish, but holy and blameless.

Tried and lost?

There is a God of new beginnings

In the preceding chapter, we saw the sovereignty of God in the lives of those who put their trust in him. Sometimes you wonder what now? after God has freed you from a life circumstance which you did not bargain for. In this context it may be the call to glory of a spouse or when the marriage ends in a divorce due to no fault of yours or the opposite. When a Christian marriage ends in a divorce, it is always very painful and hard to comprehend because these people profess their love for Christ who advocates selflessness and putting the needs of each other above theirs.

Divorce is Painful

Everyone desires "happily ever after" but sometimes, it is a struggle to make it out alive. Some do not make it out with their lives, rather they end up dead. A typical case happened in the Houston area where a deranged maniac took hostage and murdered a whole family of Eight: his ex-wife, her husband, his own son and five of the woman's children. This kind of a thing happened many times before and may continue to happen. If you made it out alive, I just want you to know that God is the one who brings a new beginning and also writes the last chapter.

Who is to be blamed?

In many cases of divorce, there may be the feeling of being a failure because, obviously, what should have lasted a lifetime did not. There may be self-blame. If the relationship was abusive in any form, there may be that feeling of low self-worth for some time. This often is as a result of having been told over and over again that you are no good and if I leave no other person will find you attractive. If we are not very careful we begin to believe this lie from the pit of hell.

Much as we need to take an honest look at ourselves and see where we may not have done right, we do not have to believe the lies that we are no good. This usually happens when we make gods out of our spouses, and let them feel that our lives are dependent on the relationship. They may not feel that way, but we may have convinced ourselves that they are. Fact of the matter is that only God is indispensable. Reiterating what we said earlier, we all have a void that only God can fill. No man or woman can fill that void. If you have given that place to a human being, please back off.

Hurting People

Those who have unresolved issues and are carrying hidden scars from early childhood are more likely to hurt others. Those who do not feel very good about themselves are more likely to make other people feel bad about themselves. That is the only way they feel good, by berating their spouses and others. They exaggerate every little shortcoming and make it a major issue; all the while, they are blind to see their own faults.

There are several reasons and for divorce as well as statistics. As stated by the Census Bureau 2009, here are some interesting facts about divorce: Age as a Factor

Couples between the age brackets of 20-24 have the most divorce rate, with 36.6% of women wanting to end their marriage, and 38.8% of men wanting to end theirs. This is followed by couples under the age of 20 years. 27.6% of women in this age bracket want to end their marriages while 11.7% of men want to end theirs. (U.S. Census Bureau, 2009)

It has also been found that couples with no children are slightly more likely to go in for a divorce than those who have children. (U.S. Census Bureau, 2009)

Vulnerable

If you have been through one, do not go into another relationship hastily, while you are still vulnerable. Find yourself once again, know your past mistakes. Do a SWAT analysis on you and know who best compliments you at this stage of your life. There are some out there who think it is their duty to take advantage of you at this moment. Do not set yourself up for another emotional roller coaster. It is interesting to know that while 41%-50% of first marriages would end in divorce, 60-67% of second marriages would break up. Third time may be the charm in other things but not in marriage as 73%-74% of third marriages will end in divorce.

The Road to Happiness

This is surely not lined with hatred. You must forgive the one who hurt you to have a high quality of life. If you do not, it is like holding someone on the ground while screaming at him or her to let you go. You are holding yourself if you have unforgiveness towards your ex spouse. Is it easy to forgive that level of betrayal? No. If you do not, they are living their lives as well as yours. It is so expensive; you simply cannot afford it. Jim Reeves wrote a song many years ago which he called "Two men and a gun" Please listen to it.

Many have found true love and happiness in the second, third or even fourth marriages. When God is in the midst of a relationship, even a toxic one can become a wholesome one.

Seek first the kingdom of God and its righteousness and these other things will be added to you. When the right person comes you will have a witness in your spirit.

My sincere desire is that this book will provoke you into thinking about what marriage is, from the biblical viewpoint. Marriage requires hard work and a lot of selflessness. While it can be challenging, it is also very fulfilling and worth fighting for. You can start by planning ahead, talking through issues, discussing your differences and putting God at the head of your home. Marriage is a beautiful thing when done right, according to the Author's manual. If not done right it can be the most toxic experience and the shortest road to hell.

Our God is a God of a new beginning and a God of a million chances.

ABOUT THE AUTHOR

Rose Enyioma is a children's Sunday school teacher. She taught Christian youth fellowship classes for several years. She continues to organize and speak at women's conferences. Her passion is geared towards strengthening and encouraging Christian homes and marriages as well as equipping young adults with Biblical skills for successful marriages. Rose is a Registered nurse and runs an independent consulting company for home health agencies.

She obtained her Bachelor's degree in Nursing from University of Nigeria, and a Master's degree in Nursing Education from Capella University, Minneapolis.

She currently lives with her husband and three children in Missouri City, Texas.

Contact Rose at: chrysolyteintegrated@yahoo.com

www.ingramcontent.com/pod-product-compliance
Lightning Source LLC
LaVergne TN
LVHW051525070426
835507LV00023B/3311